The Original

ANNABEL
FOX

*An Exclusive Knitwear
Collection*

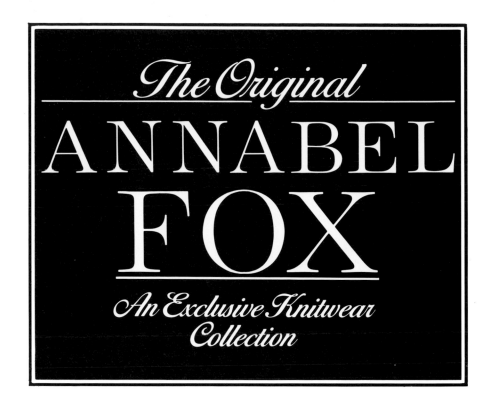

The Original
ANNABEL FOX

An Exclusive Knitwear Collection

Anaya Publishers Ltd
LONDON

First published in Great Britain in 1991
by Anaya Publishers Ltd, Strode House,
44-50 Osnaburgh Street, London NW1 3ND

Editor   Margaret Maino
Designer   David Fordham
Photographer   Ray Moller
Fashion Director and Stylist   Annabel Fox
Pattern Checker   Marilyn Wilson
Chartist   Sarah Heron
Knitting Techniques Illustrator   Conny Jude

British Library Cataloguing in Publication Data

Fox, Annabel
The original Annabel Fox
I. Title
746.43

ISBN 1-85470-021-9

Typeset in Great Britain by SX Composing Ltd, Rayleigh, Essex
Colour reproduction by Columbia Offset, Singapore
Printed and bound in China

CONTENTS

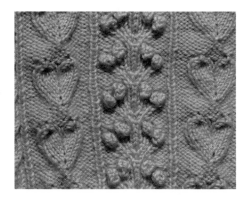

INTRODUCTION

I T SOUNDS quite strange looking back now after many years as a knitwear designer that I'm the very *first* knitter in my family . . . and that I only learned to knit at art college because I changed the direction of my degree course – a fellow student had to teach me! Those few hours being taught the basics of the craft changed my life and I'm eternally grateful that I did it.

Growing up in an army family meant that we were constantly posted all over the world – I was born in Dorset, but soon afterwards went to Hong Kong. Right from an early age I was absorbing the colours and textures of wherever I was, especially on the long hot summer holidays spent camping around the Mediterranean, painting and swimming.

Thus a career in the arts was a natural progression; two riotous years spent at Cambridge on an Art Foundation course were followed by three years studying Fashion and Textiles at Ravensbourne College of Art, Kent. My final collection was a mixture of printed textiles and hand-knits. I loved knitting from then on and set up in business with my first small collection of handknitted ·sweaters.·

This book then is the culmination of ten years' experience. It is a family knitting book, that should appeal to *all* generations. I can't see why one design shouldn't suit everyone from grandchild to grandma, if it's practicable. I think it is very important that all these designs are totally classical and not just this year's look. I want people to be happy wearing them in five to six years' time – in fact I know from experience that some of my sweaters 'improve' with age because designs that were previously sold in '85 were relaunched by demand recently and I can't make enough of them.

My other aim with this family collection was to cover the complete range of knitters' expertise with enough choice so that the youngest daughter in the family can successfully make a plain and simple garment, while the more experienced knitters such as mother or grandmother are satisfied too. In addition, none of my designs is terribly expensive to make – most use basic wool or cotton yarns rather than the more-costly luxury fibres. I am constantly being asked where I get my inspiration from. My family background of travel and textiles meant that I was brought up surrounded by the arts, crafts and influences of many different cultures. When I was still very young, I was introduced to crochet, embroidery and painting at Tildonk – a Belgian convent in the flat countryside outside Brussels that I attended for four years from the age of six.

It is impossible to underestimate the huge impact that this school – where everything was taught in French and hours of kneeling, praying and waiting for religious ceremonies were the order of the day – had on my impressionable life. Firstly it taught me patience and tolerance which are essential in knitting, but the most enjoyable part of my Tildonk schooling was its dedication to the arts – with music, ballet and needlework as key subjects in the curriculum. At 11 years I left Belgium for boarding school in England, but the skills I learned there are an important part of my background.

My mother is an experienced needlewoman who encouraged me to try crochet work, weaving, embroidery and patchwork. Really I am carrying on a tradition that goes way back in both my parents' families. My mother's family was called Fletcher: the Fletchers were famous lacemakers in the 18th century in Derbyshire, later setting up factories in Nottingham, the centre of the lace trade. The Fletcher House of Lace was a notable landmark for many years. I still have a few pieces of their silk lace in my collection.

On the paternal side, the Foxes were from Northumberland; the women were all skilled at needlecrafts. The men were mainly landowners or soldiers – my grandfathers served in the Indian Army and fought on the legendary North-West Frontier in Afghanistan.

I have always been very aware of my environment and have an almost obsessive regard to detail. Despite my colourful background I take great pains to research any design, using a wide library. I find textiles and colours irresistible in many forms, from an old brick wall in a garden or a piece of china, a postcard or a tassel border from an old Turkish rug. In the same way that I pay attention to design details, I was very particular about the photography for this book. We shot the pictures in the Languedoc region of France. I chose that area because there's such a range of locations . . . mountains, beaches, vineyards, a canal route and beautiful medieval villages . . . that reflect the light, colours and mood of my clothes. It was an incredibly creative and enjoyable experience which I think is evident when you leaf through the pages and absorb the quality of the photography.

*A washing line display shows a range of
Annabel's designs – large and small – with
their bright colours, subtle hues and rich
patterns.*

To authenticate the venture, as well as professional models, most of my family . . . nephews, nieces, mother-in-law, husband, his brother, sisters were commandeered as models. Our base was a run-down château near Narbonne on the east coast below the Pyrenees. For one shot we even borrowed a wonderful old character (see Gold Dragon on page 21) from the village, dragging him away from his game of boules. The locals were intrigued when they saw what we were doing and went out of their way to help us.

Although it has been hard work putting this book together, it has been extremely enjoyable. Hopefully, everyone who tries the designs here will grow with the book, going from one pattern to another – enjoying the test and satisfaction of making their very own garment.

The beauty of knitting is that after a bit of practice and experience, you don't have to rigidly follow the colours or plan that I've laid down – you can adapt your own ideas to make something that will always be completely your own . . . the very meaning of *unique*.

One day, I will know you, the reader, when I recognize one of the designs from this book walking towards me on the street.

Annabel Fox

Design Nº 1

Quizo

This long-line cotton sweater features deep horizontal bands of bold, bright intarsia motifs against a dramatic black background. The colourful stripe effect continues through the ribbed lower edge and cuffs.

SIZES

To fit bust 87-91[91-96:96-102]cm (34-36[36-38:38-40]in)
Actual size 124[129:134]cm (49[51:53]in)
Length to shoulder 68[70:72]cm (26¾[27½:28½]in)
Sleeve seam 43[44.5:46]cm (17[17½:18]in)
Figures in square brackets [ ] refer to larger sizes; where there is only one set of figures, it applies to all sizes

MATERIALS

13[13:14] × 50g balls of Rowan Handknit DK Cotton in main colour A (Black 252 or Scarlet 265)
2[3:3] balls in colour B (Scarlet 265 or Black 252)
1[2:2] balls in colour C (Fuchsia 258)
2[2:3] balls in colour D (Mustard 246)
1[2:2] balls in colour E (China 267)
1[2:2] balls in colour F (Clover 266)
1[1:1] ball in colour G (Violet 256)
1[2:2] balls in colour H (Bayou 279)
1[2:2] balls in colour I (Flame 254)
1[1:1] ball in colour J (Ecru 251)
1[1:2] balls in colour K (Purple 272)
Pair each of 3¼mm (US3) and 4mm (US6) knitting needles

TENSION

22 sts and 26 rows to 10cm (4in) over intarsia patt using 4mm (US6) needles

BACK

Using 3¼mm (US3) needles and B, cast on 107 [113:119] sts. Commence multi-colour rib patt, joining colours as required and stranding yarn not in use loosely across WS of work.
1st row (RS) Using B, K1, (P1, K1) to end.
2nd row Using F, K1, (P1, K1) twice, (using A, P1, using F, K1, (P1, K1) twice) to end.
3rd row Using F, P1, (K1, P1) twice, (using A, K1, using F, P1, (K1, P1) twice) to end.
4th-21st rows Rep 2nd and 3rd rows 9 times, replacing F with colours in sequence as foll: I, E, C, H, I, F, E, H, B.
22nd row Using B, P8[6:9], inc in next st, (P8[9:9], inc in next st) to last 8[6:9] sts, P to end. 118[124:130] sts.
Change to 4mm (US6) needles.
Beg with a K row, cont in st st and patt from Chart, starting at row 13[7:1]. Read odd-numbered (K) rows from right to left and even-numbered (P) rows from left to right. Strand colour not in use loosely across WS of work where appropriate or use small, separate balls of yarn for individual motifs.
Work 8[10:10] rows. Inc one st at each end of next and every foll 8th[10th:10th] row until there are 136[142:148] sts. Cont without shaping until Chart row 106 has been completed, so ending with a P row.

Shape armholes

Cast off 3 sts at beg of next 2 rows and 2 sts at beg of foll 2 rows. 126[132:138] sts.*
Cont without shaping until Chart row 170 has been completed, so ending with a P row.

Shape shoulders and back neck

Next row K18[21:24] sts, K until there are 23 sts on right-hand needle, turn and complete right side of neck.
Work one row. Cast off rem 23 sts.

Bright and beautiful, 'Quizo' is an outstanding design.

Design Nᵒ 1

'*I love the semi-abstract illustrations of birds and animals in this sweater. The interpretation of the figures into knitted fabric gives them a naïve, almost religious, quality.*

Quizo is the name of a town in Guatemala and the images are very representative of folk art in that region. To capture their original vivid colours, I have used intense, bright shades of cotton against black.'

With RS of work facing, sl centre 44 sts on to a holder, rejoin yarn to next st and K to end.
Next row Cast off 18[21:24] sts, P to end.
Work one row. Cast off rem 23 sts.

FRONT

Work as given for Back to *
Cont without shaping until Chart row 156 has been completed, so ending with a P row.

Shape neck

Next row Patt 50[53:56] sts, turn and leave rem sts on a spare needle.
Complete left side of neck first. Cast off at beg of next and foll alt rows 4 sts once, 3 sts once and one st twice. 41[44:47] sts. Cont without shaping until Chart row 170 (row 171 for other side of neck) has been completed, so ending at armhole edge.

Shape shoulder

Cast off 18[21:24] sts at beg of next row.
Work one row. Cast off rem 23 sts.
With RS of work facing, sl centre 26 sts on to a holder, rejoin yarn to next st and patt to end. Work one row, then complete as given for other side of neck, noting the bracketed exception.

SLEEVES

Using 3¼mm (US3) needles and B, cast on 53 sts. Work 21 rows in multi-colour rib patt as given for Back welt.

This sweater is a striking combination of stripes, geometric shapes and animal motifs in brilliant colours that shine out in the sunlight.

22nd row Using B, P6, inc in next st, (P9, inc in next st) to last 6 sts, P6. 58 sts.
Change to 4mm (US6) needles.
Beg with a K row, cont in st st and patt from Chart, inc one st at each end of 4th and every foll 3rd row until there are 108 sts. Cont without shaping until 94th[98th:102nd] row of Chart has been completed, so ending with a P row.

Shape top

Cast off 6 sts at beg of next 2 rows, 4 sts at beg of foll 8 rows and 9 sts at beg of next 2 rows.
Cast off rem 46 sts.

NECKBAND

Join right shoulder seam.
Using 3¼mm (US3) needles, A and with RS of work facing, pick up and K19 sts down left front neck, K across 26 sts on holder, pick up and K19 sts up right front neck, one st down right back neck, K across 44 sts on holder and pick up and K one st up left back neck. 110 sts.
Work 2.5cm (1in) in K1, P1 rib. Cast off evenly in rib.

TO MAKE UP

Press on WS using a warm iron over a damp cloth. Join left shoulder and neckband seam. Set in sleeves. Join side and sleeve seams. Press seams.

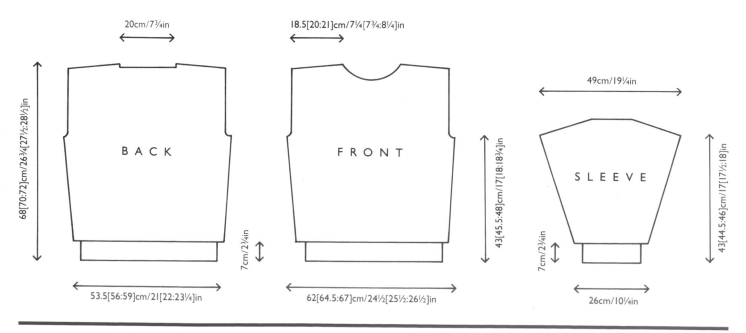

20cm/7¾in

18.5[20:21]cm/7¼[7¾:8¼]in

49cm/19¼in

68[70:72]cm/26¾[27½:28½]in

BACK

53.5[56:59]cm/21[22:23¼]in

7cm/2¾in

FRONT

43[45.5:48]cm/17[18:18¾]in

62[64.5:67]cm/24½[25½:26½]in

SLEEVE

43[44.5:46]cm/17[17½:18]in

7cm/2¾in

26cm/10¼in

Design N.º 1

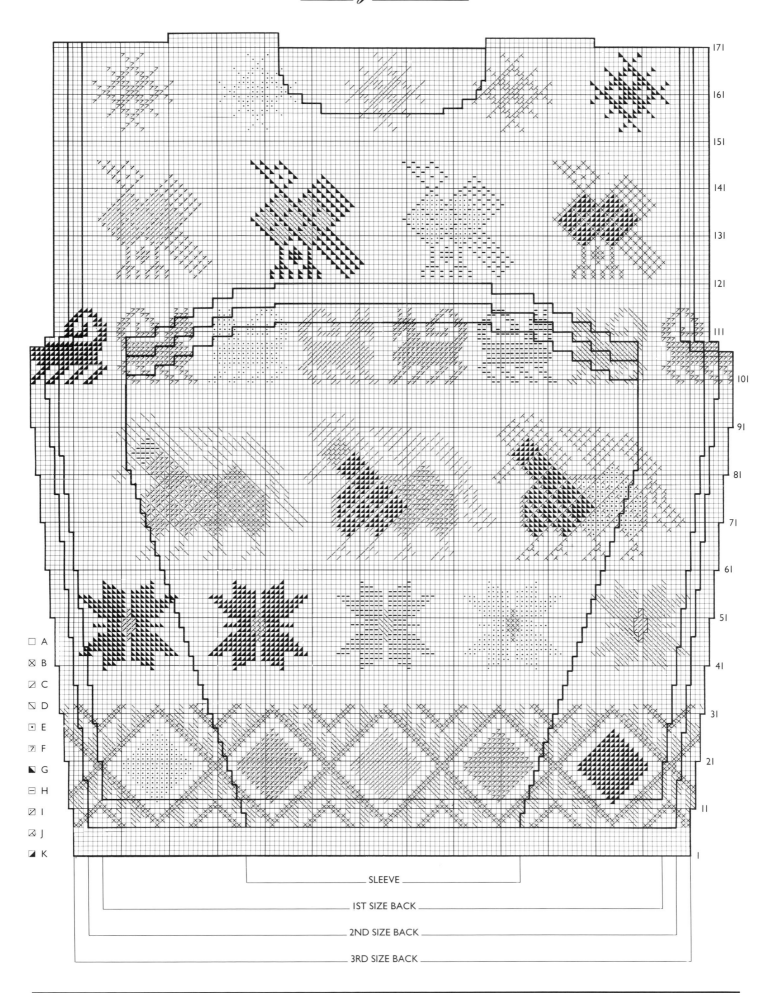

171
161
151
141
131
121
111
101
91
81
71
61
51
41
31
21
11
1

A
B
C
D
E
F
G
H
I
J
K

SLEEVE

1ST SIZE BACK

2ND SIZE BACK

3RD SIZE BACK

Dancing DEER

For the expert knitter, this is a challenging sweater to make with pairs of large and small antlered reindeer dancing across the fabric. The stylish colouring – the crisp dark cotton background with the motifs in softer wool and cotton – adds a touch of class.

SIZES

To fit chest 107[112:117]cm (42[44:46]in)
Actual size 130[134:139]cm (51[53:54½]in)
Length to shoulder 67[70:73]cm (26½[27½:28¾]in)
Sleeve seam 54.5[56:57]cm (21½[22:22½]in)
Figures in square brackets [] refer to larger sizes; where there is only one set of figures, it applies to all sizes

MATERIALS

13[13:14] × 50g balls of Rowan Cotton Glacé in main colour A (Navy 729)
5[5:6] × 40g balls of Rowan Wool and Cotton in colour B (Hazelnut 920)
7[7:8] balls of Wool and Cotton in colour C (Alabaster 909)
Pair each of 2¾mm (US2) and 3¼mm (US3) knitting needles

TENSION

28½ sts and 32 rows to 10cm (4in) over intarsia patt using 3¼mm (US3) needles

BACK

Using 2¾mm (US2) needles and A, cast on 136[144:150] sts. Work 7cm (2¾in) in K1, P1 rib, ending with a RS row.
Next row Rib 5[2:5], inc in next st, (rib 4[5:5], inc in next st) to last 5[3:6] sts, rib to end. 162[168:174] sts.
Change to 3¼mm (US3) needles.
Beg with a K row, cont in st st and patt from Chart, starting at row 21[11:1]. Read odd-numbered (K) rows from right to left and even-numbered (P) rows from left to right. Strand colour not in use loosely across WS of work where appropriate or use small, separate balls of yarn for individual motifs.
Work 8 rows. Inc one st at each end of next and every foll 8th row until there are

Mark welcomes a chance for quiet reflection. Neutral colours and subtle stonework set the scene for the restrained elegance of 'Dancing Deer'.

186[192:198] sts. Cont without shaping until Chart row 122 has been completed, so ending with a P row.

Shape armholes

Cast off 3 sts at beg of next 2 rows, 2 sts at beg of foll 2 rows and one st at beg of next 2 rows. 174[180:186] sts. *
Cont without shaping until Chart row 212 has been completed, so ending with a P row.

Shape shoulders and back neck

Next row Cast off 14[17:20] sts, K until there are 58 sts on right-hand needle, turn.
Complete right side of neck first.
**Next row Cast off 13 sts, work to end.
Next row Cast off 22 sts, work to end.
Next row Work to end.
Cast off rem 23 sts.
With RS of work facing, sl centre 30 sts on to a holder, rejoin yarn to next st and K to end.
Next row Cast off 14[17:20] sts, P to end.
Complete as given for other side of neck from ** to end.

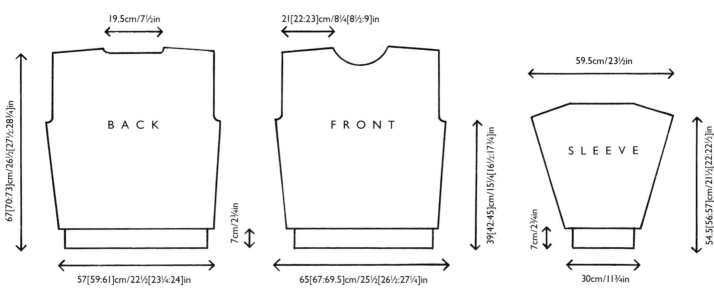

BACK — 67[70:73]cm/26½[27½:28¾]in — 19.5cm/7½in — 7cm/2¾in — 57[59:61]cm/22½[23¼:24]in

FRONT — 21[22:23]cm/8¼[8½:9]in — 39[42:45]cm/15¼[16½:17¾]in — 7cm/2¾in — 65[67:69.5]cm/25½[26½:27¼]in

SLEEVE — 59.5cm/23½in — 54.5[56:57]cm/21½[22:22½]in — 7cm/2¾in — 30cm/11¾in

Design N.º 2

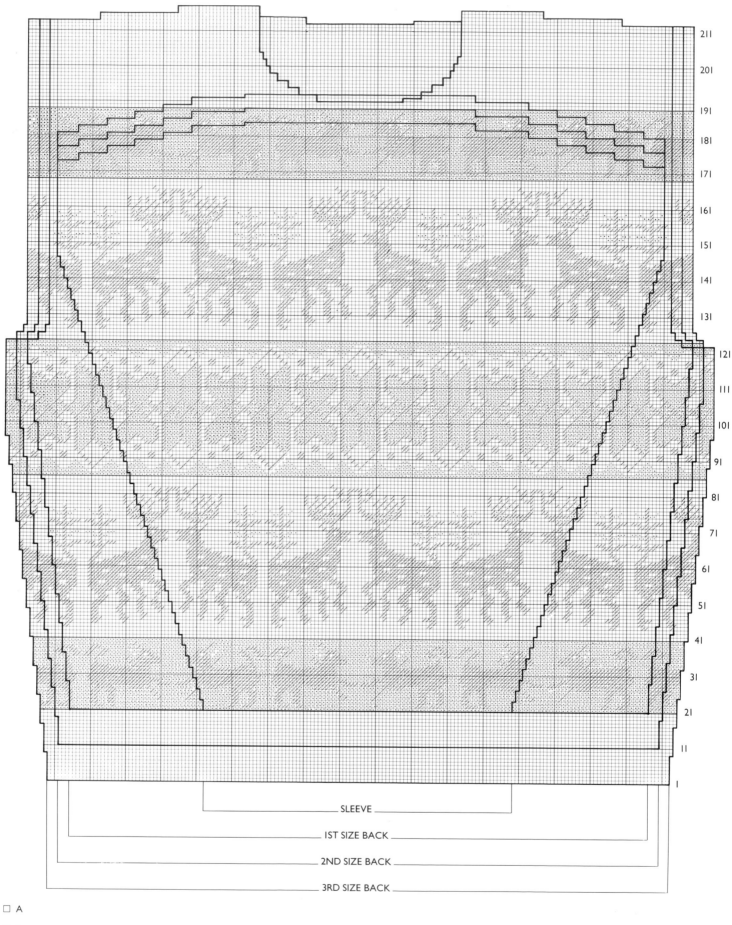

211
201
191
181
171
161
151
141
131
121
111
101
91
81
71
61
51
41
31
21
11
1

SLEEVE

1ST SIZE BACK

2ND SIZE BACK

3RD SIZE BACK

☐ A

⊡ B

▨ C

Design Nº 2

'Visiting a friend's house, I was captivated by a wall hanging that came from Turkey. The main theme of the design – these extraordinary dancing deer – is not usually associated with Mediterranean art, so to see them pop up in a design produced by Turkish peasants is quite remarkable.

In an endeavour to capture the sophisticated balance of the original design, I have been true to the patterns using lovely neutral colours against a dark navy background.'

FRONT

Work as given for Back to *.
Cont without shaping until Chart row 190 has been completed, so ending with a P row.

Shape neck

Next row K75[78:81] sts, turn and leave rem sts on a spare needle.
Complete left side of neck first. Cast off at beg of next and foll alt rows 5 sts once, 3 sts twice, 2 sts once and one st 3 times.
59[62:65] sts. Cont without shaping until Chart row 212 (row 213 for other side of neck) has been completed, so ending at armhole edge.

Shape shoulder

Cast off 14[17:20] sts at beg of next row and 22 sts at beg of foll alt row. Work one row.
Cast off rem 23 sts.
With RS of work facing, sl centre 24 sts on to a holder, rejoin yarn to next st and K to end. Work one row, then complete as given for other side of neck, noting the bracketed exception.

SLEEVES

Using 2¾mm (US2) needles and A, cast on 66 sts. Work 7cm (2¾in) in K1, P1 rib, ending with a RS row.

Next row Rib 4, inc in next st, (rib 2, inc in next st) to last 4 sts, rib 4. 86 sts.
Change to 3¼mm (US3) needles.
Beg with a K row, cont in st st and patt from Chart, inc one st at each end of 4th row and every foll 3rd row until there are 170 sts.
Cont without shaping until Chart row 172[176:180] has been completed, so ending with a P row.

Shape top

Cast off 6 sts at beg of next 2 rows, 8 sts at beg of foll 8 rows and 15 sts at beg of next 2 rows. Cast off rem 64 sts.

NECKBAND

Join right shoulder seam.
Using 2¾mm (US2) needles, A and with RS of work facing, pick up and K31 sts down left front neck, K across 24 sts on holder, pick up and K31 sts up right front neck, 13 sts down right back neck, K across 30 sts on holder and pick up and K13 sts up right back neck. 142 sts.
Work 5cm (2in) in K1, P1 rib. Cast off loosely in rib.

TO MAKE UP

Press on WS using a warm iron over a damp cloth. Join left shoulder and neckband seams. Fold neckband in half to inside and slip stitch in position. Join side and sleeve seams. Press seams.

The bands of pattern continue across the back of the sweater to make a busy intricate fabric that is a delight to look at.

15

Design Nº 3

Ming

This is an outsize loose sweater for cool summer wear. Knitted in a cotton chenille yarn, the intarsia pattern features a bold dragon design in dramatic Oriental colours. A knitted lace border at the hem is trimmed with optional crochet bobbles and tassels.

SIZES

To fit bust 87-91[91-96:102-107]cm (34-36[36-38:40-42]in)
Actual size 126[132:138]cm (49½[52:54]in)
Length to shoulder 65.5[68:71]cm (25¾[26¾:28]in)
Sleeve seam 42.5[42.5:44]cm (16¾[16¾:17¼]in)
Figures in square brackets [] refer to larger sizes; where there is only one set of figures, it applies to all sizes.

MATERIALS

Colourway A
18[19:19] × 50g balls of Rowan DK Cotton in main colour A (True Navy 244)
1 ball of DK Cotton in each of 2 colours B (Snow Thistle 288) and C (Sky 264)
1 × 50g ball of Rowan Fine Chenille in each of colours D (Box 393) and E (Mole 380)
1× 50g ball of Rowan Sea Breeze in colour F (Polka 530 – use double throughout)
1 ball of DK Cotton in colour G (Lilac 269)

1 ball of Fine Chenille in each of 2 colours H (Plum 386) and I (Lacquer 388)
Colourway B
18[19:19] × 50g balls of Rowan DK Cotton in main colour A (Cherry 298)
1 ball of DK Cotton in each of 8 colours B (True Navy 244), C (Sunflower 261), D (Purple 272), E (Azure 248), F (Port 245), G (China 267), H (Royal 294), and I (Kingfisher 273)
Pair of 4mm (US6) knitting needles
3.50mm (US E/4) crochet hook

TENSION

22 sts and 28 rows to 10cm (4in) over patt using 4mm (US6) needles

BACK

Using 4mm (US6) needles and A, cast on 15 sts for lace border. K one row. Cont in patt from Lace Border Chart, reading odd-numbered (RS) rows from right to left and even-numbered (WS) rows from left to right. Rep the 44 rows of patt 4 times in all shaping lower edge as shown, by dec one st at beg of 1st row, then inc one st at beg of 11 foll alt rows, then dec one st at beg of next 10 alt rows. Cast off 15 sts.
Using 4mm (US6) needles, A and with RS of work facing, pick up and K138[146:152] sts along top edge of lace border. P one row.

Although Annabel wears 'Ming' to cover up on a summer's day, she will never be in the shade with this dramatic design. The knitted lace cuffs and hem accentuated with tassels make a bold feature.

Design Nº 3

1ST SIZE BACK

2ND SIZE BACK

3RD SIZE BACK

*'I frequently travel to Hong Kong in my role as a knitwear designer. The
dragon symbol sums up the world of the East: it is used everywhere.
My own interest in the dragon began when my son was born in the Year of
the Dragon – the most prestigious and fortuitous of the Chinese calendar.'*

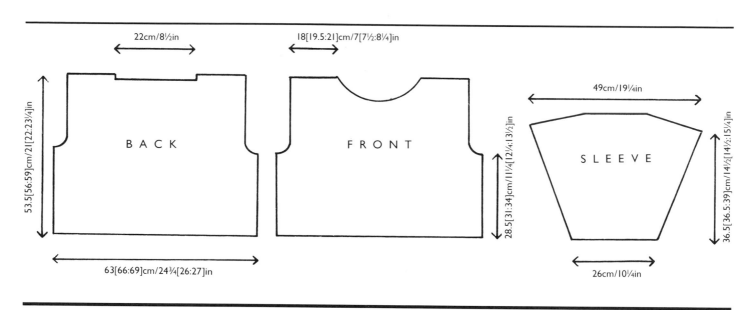

Beg with a K row, cont in st st and patt from Chart, starting at row 17[9:1]. Strand colour not in use loosely across WS of work where appropriate or use small, separate balls of yarn for individual motifs. Cont in patt until Chart row 96 has been completed, so ending with a P row.

Shape armholes
Cast off 3 sts at beg of next 2 rows, 2 sts at beg of foll 2 rows and one st at beg of next 2 rows. 126[134:140] sts. *
Cont without shaping until Chart row 166 has been completed, so ending with a P row.

Shape shoulders and back neck
Next row Cast off 20[22:23] sts, patt until there are 19[21:23] sts on right-hand needle, turn and complete right side of neck first.
Work one row. Cast off rem sts.
With RS of work facing, rejoin yarn to next st, cast off centre 48 sts, patt to end.
Next row Cast off 20[22:23] sts, patt to end. Work one row. Cast off rem 19[21:23] sts.

FRONT

Work as given for Back to *.
Cont without shaping until Chart row 150 has been completed, so ending with a P row.

Shape neck
Next row Patt 55[59:62] sts, turn and complete left side of neck first.
**Cast off at beg of next and foll alt rows 6 sts once, 4 sts once, 3 sts once, 2 sts once and one st once. 39[43:46] sts.
Cont without shaping until Chart row 166 (row 167 for other side of neck) has been completed, so ending at armhole edge.

Shape shoulder
Cast off 20[22:23] sts at beg of next row.
Work one row. Cast off rem 19[21:23] sts.
With RS of work facing, rejoin yarn to next st, cast off centre 16 sts, patt to end. Work one row, then complete as given for other side of neck from ** to end, noting the bracketed exception.

SLEEVES

Using 4mm (US6) needles and A, cast on 8 sts. K one row. Commence cuff patt.
1st row (WS) P1, K2, yfwd, sl next 2 sts K-wise, one at a time, then insert the tip of the left-hand needle into the fronts of these sts from the left and K them tog – called ssk, K1, (yo) twice, (yo) twice, K1.
2nd row (K1, K1 then P1 into yo twice of previous row) twice, K2, P1, K3.
3rd row P1, K2, yfwd, ssk, K7.
4th row Cast off 4 sts, K4 including st used to cast off, P1, K3.
Rep these 4 rows to form patt. Cont in patt until cuff measures 26 cm (10¼in) from beg, ending with a 4th row. Cast off.
Using 4mm (US6) needles, A and with RS of work facing, pick up and K58 sts along top edge of cuff. P one row.
Beg with a K row, cont in st st and patt from Chart, inc one st at each end of 4th and every foll 3rd row until there are 108 sts. Cont without shaping until 102[102:106] rows have been completed, so ending with a P row.

Shape top
Cast off 5 sts at beg of next 2 rows, 4 sts at beg of foll 10 rows and 7 sts at beg of next 2 rows. Cast off rem 44 sts.

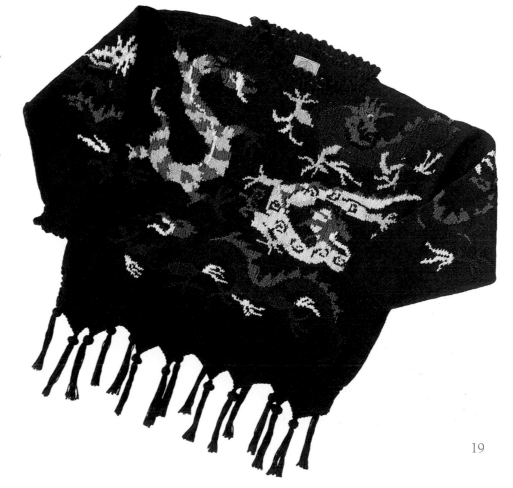

Design N.º 3

SLEEVE

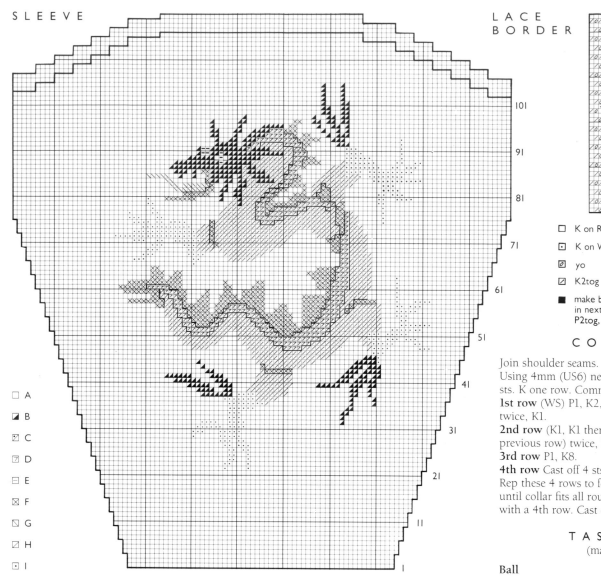

- □ A
- ◪ B
- ⊡ C
- ▨ D
- ⊟ E
- ⊠ F
- ◩ G
- ▨ H
- ⊡ I

LACE BORDER

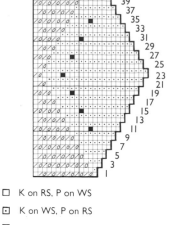

- □ K on RS, P on WS
- ⊡ K on WS, P on RS
- ▨ yo
- ▧ K2tog
- ■ make bobble – (K1, yo) twice, K1 all in next st, turn P5, turn K5, turn P2tog, P1, P2tog, turn sl 1, K2tog, psso.

COLLAR

Join shoulder seams.

Using 4mm (US6) needles and A, cast on 5 sts. K one row. Commence patt.

1st row (WS) P1, K2, (yo) twice, K1, (yo) twice, K1.

2nd row (K1, K1 then P1 into yo twice of previous row) twice, K3.

3rd row P1, K8.

4th row Cast off 4 sts, K to end.

Rep these 4 rows to form patt. Cont in patt until collar fits all round neck edge, ending with a 4th row. Cast off.

TASSELS
(make 16)

Ball

Using 3.50mm (US E/4) crochet hook and A, make 2ch.

1st round Work 8dc into 2nd ch from hook.

2nd round Work 2dc into each dc to end. 16dc.

3rd round (Miss 1dc, 1dc into next dc) to end. 8dc.

Cut off yarn, leaving a long end. Thread cut end through each of 8 sts and leave to pull up tight later.

Fringe

Cut 7 × 33cms (13in) lengths of yarn. Insert crochet hook through centre of ball and draw fringe (folded in half) through. Use end of yarn from working initial ch to sew end of fringe in position inside ball. At the opposite end, draw up thread and fasten off.

TO MAKE UP

Press on WS to work using a warm iron over a damp cloth. Set in sleeves. Join side and sleeve seams. Press seams. Sew on 8 tassels to points of lace border, with 8 more between.

Three versions of 'Ming' – Amanda (left) in plain navy, Brigit (centre) in vivid red and Monica (right) in the navy patterned version.

GOLD
Dragon

Knitted in stocking stitch and Rowan Designer DK, this sweater has an eye-catching bold dragon pattern in a glittering yarn against a dramatic black background.

SIZES

To fit chest 96-102[102-107:107-112]cm (38-40[40-42:42-44]in)
Actual size 127[134:140]cm (50[53:55]in)
Length to shoulder 71.5[74:77]cm (28¼[29:30¼]in)
Sleeve seam 41.5[41.5:42.5]cm (16¼[16¼:16¾]in)
Figures in square brackets [] refer to larger sizes; where there is only one set of figures, it applies to all sizes

MATERIALS

12[13:14] × 50g balls of Rowan Designer DK in main colour A (black 62)
1 cone (110g) of Texere White Gold (colour B – use double)
Pair each of 3¼mm (US3) and 4mm (US6) knitting needles

TENSION

22 sts and 30 rows to 10cm (4in) over st st using Designer DK and 4mm (US6) needles

FRONT

Using 3¼mm (US3) needles and A, cast on 110[118:122] sts.
1st row (K1 tbl, P1) to end.
Rep this row to form twisted rib until work measures 5cm (2in) from beg, ending with a RS row.
Next row Rib 7[6:3], inc in next st, (rib 4, inc in next st) to last 7[6:3] sts, rib to end. 130[140:146] sts.
Change to 4mm (US6) needles.
Beg with a K row, cont in st st and patt from Chart, starting at row 15[9:1]. Read odd-numbered (K) rows from right to left and even-numbered (P) rows from left to right. Strand colour not in use loosely across WS of work where appropriate or use small, separate balls of yarn for individual motifs.

Annabel proves that her sweater looks just as good on a woman as it does on a man.

Overleaf A typical Gallic character proudly models the same 'Golden Dragon' sweater.

Work 10 rows. Inc one st at each end of next and every foll 10th row until there are 148[158:164] sts. Cont without shaping until Chart row 126 has been completed, so ending with a P row.

Shape armholes

Cast off 3 sts at beg of next 2 rows, 2 sts at beg of foll 2 rows and one st at beg of next 2 rows. 136[146:152] sts. Cont without shaping until Chart row 186 has been completed, so ending with a P row.

Shape neck

Next row Patt 60[65:68] sts, turn and leave rem sts on a spare needle.
Cast off at beg of next and foll alt rows 4 sts 3 times, 2 sts once and one st once. 45[50:53] sts.
Cont without shaping until Chart row 202 (row 203 for other side of neck) has been completed, so ending at armhole edge.

Shape shoulder

Cast off 25[27:27] sts at beg of next row. Work one row. Cast off rem 20[23:26] sts.
With RS of work facing, sl centre 16 sts on to a holder, rejoin yarn to next st and patt to end. Work one row, then complete as given for other side of neck.

BACK

Using 3¼mm (US3) needles and A, cast on 100[118:122] sts. Work 5cm (2in) in twisted rib as given for Front welt, ending with a RS row.
Next row Rib 5[9:8], inc in next st, (rib 8[8:7], inc in next st) to last 5[9:9] sts, rib to end. 122[130:136] sts.
Change to 4mm (US6) needles.
Beg with a K row, cont in st st, inc one st at each end of 11th and every foll 10th row until there are 140[148:154] sts. Cont without shaping until Back measures same as Front to underarms, ending with a P row.

Shape armholes

Cast off 3 sts at beg of next 2 rows, 2 sts at beg of foll 2 rows and one st at beg of next 2 rows. 128[136:142] sts. Cont without shaping until Back measures same as Front to shoulders, ending with a P row.

Shape shoulders and back neck

Next row Cast off 23[25:25] sts, K until there are 19[21:24] sts on right-hand needle, turn. Work one row. Cast off rem 19[21:24] sts.

Design Nº 4

201
191
181
171
161
151
141
131
121
111
101
91
81
71
61
51
41
31
21
11
1

☐ A

☒ B

1ST SIZE FRONT

2ND SIZE FRONT

3RD SIZE FRONT

Design N° 4

'When I was a child we lived in Hong Kong and to my impressionable young eyes it was a magical city. Even today when I return there on business, I still wonder at the exotic quality that is the essence of the East.
The dragon is a very strong symbol in Oriental art; to maintain that strength I have only used the pattern on the front of the sweater, keeping the back and sleeves in a plain colour.'

With RS of work facing, sl centre 44 sts on to a holder, rejoin yarn to next st and K to end.
Next row Cast off 23[25:25] sts, P to end. Work one row. Cast off rem 19[21:24] sts.

SLEEVES

Using 3¼mm (US3) needles and A, cast on 48 sts. Work 5cm (2in) in twisted rib as given for Front welt, ending with a RS row.
Next row Rib 4, inc in next st, (rib 2, inc in next st) to last 4 sts, rib 4. 62 sts.
Change to 4mm (US6) needles.
Beg with a K row, cont in st st, inc one st at each end of 5th and every foll 3rd row until there are 122 sts. Cont without shaping until work measures 41.5[41.5:42.5]cm (16¼[16¼:16¾]in) from beg, ending with a P row.

Shape top

Cast off 8 sts at beg of next 2 rows, 4 sts at beg of foll 12 rows and 10 sts at beg of next 2 rows. Cast off rem 38 sts.

NECKBAND

Join right shoulder seam.
Using 3¼mm (US3) needles, A and with RS of work facing, pick up and K23 sts down left front neck, K across 16 sts on holder, pick up and K23 sts up right front neck, one st down right back neck, K across 44 sts on holder and pick up and K one st up left back neck. 108 sts. Work 6cm (2½in) in twisted rib. Cast off loosely in rib.

TO MAKE UP

Press on WS using a warm iron over a damp cloth. Join left shoulder and neckband seam. Fold neckband in half to inside and slip stitch in position. Set in sleeves. Join side and sleeve seams. Press seams.

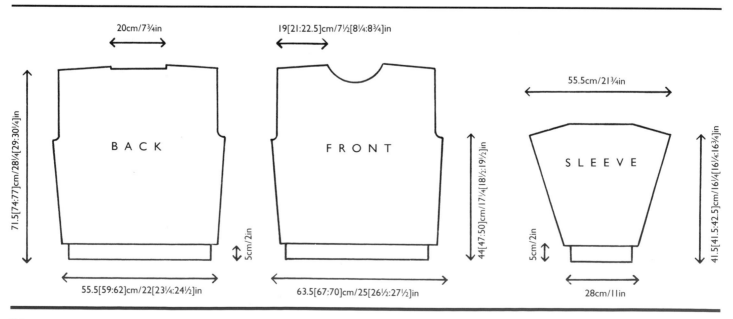

20cm/7¾in

19[21:22.5]cm/7½[8¼:8¾]in

55.5cm/21¾in

71.5[74:77]cm/28¼[29:30¼]in

BACK

5cm/2in

55.5[59:62]cm/22[23¼:24½]in

FRONT

44[47:50]cm/17¼[18½:19½]in

63.5[67:70]cm/25[26½:27½]in

SLEEVE

41.5[41.5:42.5]cm/16¼[16¼:16¾]in

5cm/2in

28cm/11in

Design N° 5

Thurso

A large range of sizes makes the Thurso collection – a sweater and cardigan plus a man's waistcoat – a family affair. The numerous and subtle shades of Rowan's Designer DK and Fox Tweed yarns are perfect for the snowflake design that is one of the most distinctive motifs in Fair Isle knitting.

SIZES

Sweater and Cardigan
To fit chest/bust 61[66:71-76:81-87:91-96:96-102:102-107:107-112:112-117]cm (24[26-28-30:32-34:36-38:38-40:40-42:42-44:44-46]in)
Actual size
65[73:90:93:108:113:120:123:128]cm
(25½[28¾:35½:36½:42½:44½:47:48½:50]in)
Length to shoulder
37[40:44:49:56:58:61:69:71]cm
(14½[15¾:17¼:19¼:22:22¾:24:27:27¾]in)

Sleeve seam 22[24:28:32:43:44:44:52:52]cm
(8½[9½:11:12½:17:17¼:17¼:20½:20½]in)

Waistcoat
To fit chest 96[102:107]cm (38[40:42]in)
Actual size 104.5[111.5:117.5]cm
(41[43¾:46¼]in)
Length to shoulder 60[64:66]cm
(23½[25:25¾]in)
Figures in square brackets [] refer to larger sizes; where there is only one set of figures, it applies to all sizes

MATERIALS

Child's Sweater and Cardigan (first 4 sizes)
2[2:3:3] × 50g balls of Rowan Designer DK in main shade A (midnight blue 671)
1[1:2:2] balls in shade B (ruby 673)
1[1:1:1] ball in shade C (chestnut 662)
1[1:1:2] balls in shade D (brown 663)
1[1:2:2] balls in shade E (mauve 652)
1[1:1:1] ball in shade F (jade 661)
1[1:1:2] balls in shade G (honey 675)
1[1:1:1] ball in shade H (pale green 664)
1[1:1:1] ball in shade I (blue 672)

Ladies'/Men's Sweater and Cardigan (last 5 sizes)
4[4:5:5:6] × 50g balls of Rowan Fox Tweed in main shade A (Wren 850)
2[3:3:3:4] × 50g balls of Rowan Designer DK in shade B (buff 616)
1[1:1:2:2] balls of Designer DK in shade C (plum 657)
2[2:3:3:3] balls of Designer DK in shade D (airforce 65)
2[2:3:3:3] × 50g balls of Rowan Lambswool Tweed in shade E (Wine Berry 181)
1[1:1:2:2] balls of Designer DK in shade F (sage 669)
2[2:3:3:3] balls of Designer DK in shade G (ecru 649)
1[1:1:1:1] ball of Designer DK in shade H (red oxide 663)
1[1:1:1:1] ball of Designer DK in shade I (deep gold 650)

Men's Waistcoat
3[3:4] × 50g balls of Rowan Fox Tweed in main shade A (Wren 850)
2[2:3] balls of Fox Tweed in shade B (Cricket 851)
1[1:1] × 50g ball of Rowan Lambswool Tweed in shade C (Wine Berry 181)
1[2:2] balls of Fox Tweed in shade D (Hare 853)
2[2:2] balls of Lambswool Tweed in shade E (Kohl 185)

Design N°5

CHART I

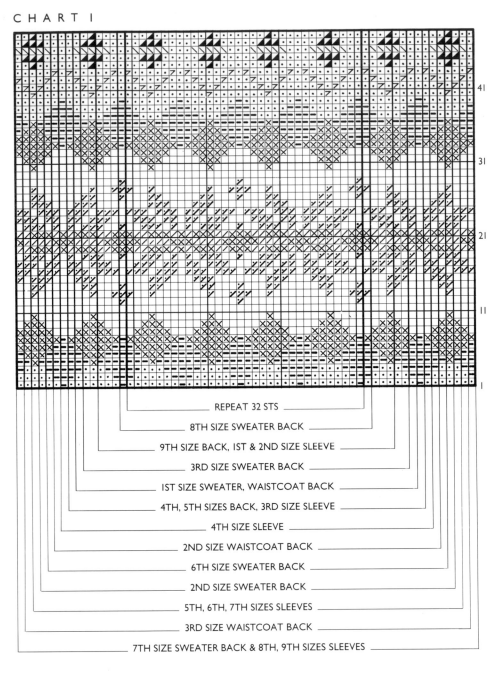

41
31
21
11
1

REPEAT 32 STS
8TH SIZE SWEATER BACK
9TH SIZE BACK, 1ST & 2ND SIZE SLEEVE
3RD SIZE SWEATER BACK
1ST SIZE SWEATER, WAISTCOAT BACK
4TH, 5TH SIZES BACK, 3RD SIZE SLEEVE
4TH SIZE SLEEVE
2ND SIZE WAISTCOAT BACK
6TH SIZE SWEATER BACK
2ND SIZE SWEATER BACK
5TH, 6TH, 7TH SIZES SLEEVES
3RD SIZE WAISTCOAT BACK
7TH SIZE SWEATER BACK & 8TH, 9TH SIZES SLEEVES

□ A	☑ D	☒ G
☒ B	⊡ E	☐ H
⊟ C	◪ F	◩ I

1[1:1] ball of Fox Tweed in shade F (Seal 852)
1[2:2] × 50g balls of Rowan Designer DK in shade G (red oxide 663)
1[1:1] ball of Designer DK in shade H (sage 669)
1[1:1] ball of Designer DK in shade I (pale green 664)
Pair each of 3¼mm (US3) and 4mm (US6) knitting needles
5[5:6:6:5:5:6:7:8] buttons for Cardigan
5[6:7] buttons for Waistcoat

TENSION

24 sts and 25 rows to 10cm (4in) over Fair Isle patt using 4mm (US6) needles

26

SWEATER

BACK

Using 3¼mm (US3) needles and A, cast on 70[76:100:100:94:96:102:110:114] sts. Work 1 row K1, P1 rib. Cont in rib and stripe sequence of 2 rows each of B, C, D, E, F, G and H until work measures 6cm (2½in) from beg, ending with a RS row.
Next row Rib 7[5:7:5:4:6:4:7:4], inc in next st, (rib 7[5:11:7:4:3:3:4:4], inc in next st) to last 6[4:8:6:4:5:5:7:4] sts, rib to end. 78[88:108:112:112:118:126:130:136] sts. Change to 4mm (US6) needles.
Beg with a K row, cont in st st and fair isle

patt from Chart 1, reading odd-numbered (K) rows from right to left and even-numbered (P) rows from left to right. Weave in shades not in use into WS of work.

Last 5 sizes only
Cont in patt, inc one st at each end of 7th[7th:9th:9th:11th] row and every foll 6th[6th:8th:8th:10th] rows until there are 130[136:144:148:154] sts.

All sizes
Cont in patt without shaping until work measures 23[26:29:33:33:35:38:44:46]cm (9[10¼:11½:13:13:13¾:15:17¼:18]in) from beg, ending with a WS row.

Shape armholes
Keeping patt correct, cast off 3 sts at beg of next 2 rows and 2 sts at beg of foll 2 rows. 68[78:98:102:120:126:134:138:144] sts. *
Cont without shaping until armholes measure 13[14:15:16:23:23:23:25:25]cm (5[5½:5¾:6¼:9:9:9:9¾:9¾]in) from beg, ending with a WS row.

Shape shoulders and back neck
Next row Cast off 0[10:15:16:19:21:23:24:25] sts, patt until there are 17[10:15:16:19:20:22:23:25] sts, turn and complete right side of neck first.
Work one row. Cast off rem 17[10:15:16:19:20:22:23:25] sts.
With RS of work facing, sl centre 34[38:38:38:44:44:44:44:44] sts on to a holder (for Cardigan or Waistcoat, rejoin yarn and cast off these sts), rejoin yarn to next st and patt to end.
Next row Cast off 0[10:15:16:19:21:23:24:25] sts, patt to end.
Work one row. Cast off rem 17[10:15:16:19:20:22:23:25] sts.

FRONT

Work as given for Back to *.
Cont without shaping until armholes measure 9[9:9:10:17:17:17:18:18]cm (3½[3½:3½:4:6½:6½:6½:7:7]in) from beg, ending with a WS row.

Shape neck
Next row Patt 26[33:43:45:53:56:60:62:65] sts, turn and leave rem sts on a spare needle. Complete left side of neck first. Cast off at beg of next and foll alt rows 5[5:5:5:6:6:6:6:6] sts once, 2[4:3:3:3:3:3:3:3] sts once, 2 sts once, 0[2:2:2:2:2:2:2:2] sts once, 0[0:1:1:1:1:1:1:1] st once and 0[0:0:0:1:1:1:1:1] st once.
17[20:30:32:38:41:45:47:50] sts. Cont without shaping until Front matches Back to shoulder, ending at armhole edge.

The family wears their 'Thurso' designs. Various colourways for the garments are deceptive for they appear to be different patterns, yet the same Fair Isle motif is used throughout.

CHART 2

Design № 5

Shape shoulder

Cast off 0[10:15:16:19:21:23:24:25] sts at beg of next row. Work one row. Cast off rem 17[10:15:16:19:20:22:23:25] sts.
With RS of work facing, sl centre 16[12:12:12:14:14:14:14:14] sts on to a holder, rejoin yarn to next st and patt to end. Work one row, then complete as given for other side of neck.

SLEEVES

Using 3¼mm (US3) needles and A, cast on 36[36:42:44:48:48:48:52:52] sts. Work 6cm (2½in) in rib and stripe sequence as given for Back welt, ending with a RS row.
Next row Rib 4[4:3:4:5:5:5:3:3], inc in next st, (rib 8[8:6:6:3:3:3:4:4], inc in next st) to last 4[4:3:4:6:6:6:3:3] sts, rib to end.
40[40:48:50:58:58:58:62:62] sts.
Change to 4mm (US6) needles.
Beg with a K row, cont in st st and patt from Chart 1, inc one st at each end of 3rd[3rd:3rd:3rd:4th:4th:4th:4th:4th] row and every foll 3rd row until there are 64[64:74:82:112:112:112:122:122] sts, working extra sts into patt. Cont without shaping until Sleeve measures 22[24:28:32:43:44:44:52:52]cm (8½[9½:11:12½:17:17¼:17¼:20½:20½]in) from beg, ending with a WS row.

Shape top

Cast off 3[3:4:4:8:8:8:8:8] sts at beg of next 2 rows, 3[3:4:4:6:6:6:6:6] sts at beg of foll 8[8:8:6:6:6:6:6:6] rows and 0[0:0:8:10:10:10:10:10] sts at beg of next 2 rows. Cast off rem 34[34:34:34:40:40:40:50:50] sts.

NECKBAND

Join right shoulder seam.
Using 3¼mm (US3) needles, A and with RS of work facing, pick up and K13[18:18:18:20:20:20:22:22] sts down left front neck, K across 16[12:12:12:14:14:14:14:14] sts on holder, pick up and K13[18:18:18:20:20:20:22:22] sts up right front neck, one st down right back neck, K across 34[38:38:38:44:44:44:44:44] back neck sts on holder and pick up and K one st up left back neck.
78[88:88:88:100:100:100:104:104] sts.
Work one row in K1, P1 rib. Cont in rib and stripe sequence as given for Back welt until neckband measures 6cm (2½in) from beg.
Cast off loosely in rib.

TO MAKE UP

Press on WS of work using a warm iron over a damp cloth. Join left shoulder and neckband seam. Fold neckband in half to inside and slip stitch in position. Set in sleeves. Join side and sleeve seams.

CARDIGAN

BACK

Work as given for Back of Sweater.

28

LREPEAT 32 STS

9TH SIZE LEFT FRONT CARDIGAN

1ST SIZE LEFT FRONT CARDIGAN

2ND SIZE LEFT FRONT CARDIGAN

3RD SIZE LEFT FRONT CARDIGAN

1ST SIZE LEFT FRONT WAISTCOAT

4TH, 5TH SIZES LEFT FRONT CARDIGAN

2ND SIZE LEFT FRONT WAISTCOAT

6TH SIZE LEFT FRONT CARDIGAN

3RD SIZE LEFT FRONT WAISTCOAT

7TH SIZE LEFT FRONT CARDIGAN AND 3RD SIZE WAISTCOAT

8TH SIZE LEFT FRONT CARDIGAN

□ A	☑ D	☑ G
☒ B	· E	☷ H
☰ C	◪ F	◩ I

LEFT FRONT

Using 3¼mm (US3) needles and A, cast on 32[35:47:47:44:46:48:52:54] sts. Work 6cm (2½in) in rib and stripe sequence as given for Back welt, ending with a RS row.
Next row Rib 3[5:7:5:6:4:2:3:6], inc in next st, (rib 7[4:10:6:3:3:3:4:3], inc in next st) to last 4[4:6:6:5:5:1:3:7] sts, rib to end.
36[41:51:53:53:56:60:62:65] sts.
Change to 4mm (US6) needles.
Beg with a K row, cont in st st and Fair Isle patt from Chart 2.

Last 5 sizes only

Cont in patt, inc one st at beg (for Right Front, read 'end' here) of

7th[7th:9th:9th:11th] row and every foll 6th[6th:8th:8th:10th] row until there are 62[65:69:71:74] sts.

All sizes

Cont in patt without shaping until work measures 23[26:29:30:27:29:32:40:42]cm (9[10¼:11½:11¾:10¾:11½:12½:15¾:16½]in) from beg, ending with a WS row.

Shape armhole and front edge

Dec one st at end (for Right Front, read 'beg' here) – front edge – of next and every foll alt[next:alt:alt:alt:alt:3rd:3rd] row, *at the same time* when work measures

buttons with pins – the first to come 2cm (¾in) above lower edge and the last level with start of shaping, with the others evenly spaced between.

BUTTONHOLE BAND

Work as given for Button Band, making buttonholes as markers are reached as foll:
Buttonhole row (RS) Rib 3, yo, K2 tog, rib 2. Sew band in position, joining seam at centre back neck.

TO MAKE UP

Press on WS of work using a warm iron over a damp cloth. Set in sleeves. Join side and sleeve seams. Press seams. Sew on buttons.

WAISTCOAT

BACK

Using 3¼mm (US3) needles and A, cast on 100[104:112] sts. Work 6cm (2½in) in rib and stripe sequence as given for welt on Back of Sweater, ending with a RS row.
Next row Rib 4[8:6], inc in next st, (rib 9[7:8], inc in next st) to last 5[7:6] sts, rib to end. 110[116:124] sts.
Change to 4mm (US6) needles.
Beg with a K row, cont in st st and Fair Isle patt from Chart 2, reading odd-numbered (K) rows from right to left and even-numbered (P) rows from left to right. Weave shades not in use across WS of work. Inc one st at each end of 9th and every foll 8th row until there are 128[134:142] sts, working extra sts into patt. Cont without shaping until work measures 37[39:41]cm (14½[15¼:16]in) from beg, ending with a WS row.

23[26:29:33:33:35:38:44:46]cm (9[10¼:11½:13:13:13¾:15:17¼:18]in) from beg, ending at side edge, work as foll:

Shape armhole

Cont to dec at front edge as before, cast off 3 sts at beg of next row and 2 sts at beg of foll alt row. Keeping armhole edge straight, cont to dec at front edge only until 17[20:30:32:38:41:45:47:50] sts rem. Work straight until Front matches Back to shoulder, ending at armhole edge.

Shape shoulder

Cast off 0[10:15:16:19:21:23:24:25] sts at beg of next row. Work one row. Cast off rem 17[10:15:16:19:20:22:23:25] sts.

RIGHT FRONT

Work as given for Left Front, noting the bracketed exceptions and reversing the Chart by reading odd-numbered (K) rows from left to right and even-numbered (P) rows from right to left.

SLEEVES

Work as given for Sleeves of Sweater.

BUTTON BAND

(Right Front for boys/men, Left Front for girls/ladies)
Join shoulder seams.
Using 3¼mm (US3) needles and A, cast on 7 sts.
1st row (RS) K1, (P1, K1) to end.
2nd row Using B, P1, (K1, P1) to end.

Rep these 2 rows to form rib, *at the same time* working stripe sequence as given for Back welt until band measures 6cm (2½in). Then cont in A only until band when slightly stretched, fits up front edge and around to centre back neck. Cast off.
Sew band in position. Mark positions of

Design N°5

'Popularized by the Prince of Wales in the 1920s, the colourful patterns of Fair Isle designs are perhaps one of the most popular of the traditional knitting styles.
Fair Isle is the most southerly island of the Shetland group: the knitting skills and patterns are suppposed to originate from Spanish sailors shipwrecked there in the late 16th century. With such an interesting history I never cease to be inspired, especially with the subtle colours of true Fair Isle patterns that conjure up the wild beauty of these remote islands.'

Shape armholes

Cast off 8 sts at beg of next 2 rows. Dec one st at each end of next and every foll alt row until 90[96:104] sts rem. Cont without shaping until armholes measure 23[25:25]cm (9[9¾:9¾]in) from beg, ending with a WS row.

Shape shoulders and back neck

Next row Cast off 8[9:11] sts, patt until there are 20[22:24] sts on right-hand needle, turn and complete right side of neck first.
* **Next row** Cast off 2 sts, patt to end.
Next row Cast off 9[10:11] sts, patt to end.
Next row Patt to end. Cast off rem 9[10:11] sts. With RS of work facing, rejoin yarn to rem sts, cast off centre 34 sts, patt to end.
Next row Cast off 8[9:11] sts, patt to end.
Complete as given for other side of neck from * to end.

William, wearing his 'Thurso' cardigan, plays a game of hide and seek. This design can also be knitted as a sweater or an adult-size waistcoat. The sweater and cardigan are available in enough sizes to suit everyone in the family.

LEFT FRONT

Using 3¼mm (US3) needles and A, cast on 46[48:52] sts. Work 6cm (2½in) in rib and stripe sequence as given for Back welt, ending with a RS row.
Next row Rib 5, inc in next st, (rib 6[5:6], inc in next st) to last 5[6:4] sts, rib to end. 52[55:59] sts.
Change to 4mm (US6) needles.
Beg with K row, cont in st st and patt from Chart, inc one st at beg (for Right Front, read 'end' here) of 9th and every foll 8th row until there are 61[64:68] sts. Cont without shaping until work measures 30[32:34]cm (11¾[12½:13¼]in) from beg, ending with a RS row (end with a WS row here for Right Front).

Shape front edge

Dec one st at beg of next and every foll 4th row until work measures 37[39:41]cm (14½[15¼:16]in) from beg, ending with a WS row (end with a RS row here for Right Front).

Shape armhole

Cont to dec at front edge as before, *at the same time* cast off 10 sts at beg of next row then dec one st at beg of every foll alt row 9 times in all.
Keeping armhole edge straight, cont to dec at front edge only until 26[29:33] sts rem. Cont without shaping until Front matches Back to shoulder, ending at armhole edge.

Shape shoulder

Cast off 8[9:11] sts at beg of next row and 9[10:11] sts at beg of foll alt row. Work one row. Cast off rem 9[10:11] sts.

RIGHT FRONT

Work as given for Left Front, noting the bracketed exceptions and reversing the Chart by reading odd-numbered (K) rows from left to right and even-numbered (P) rows from right to left.

BUTTON BAND

Work as given for Button Band of Cardigan.

BUTTONHOLE BAND

Work as given for Buttonhole Band of Cardigan.

ARMBANDS

Using 3¼mm (US3) needles, A and with RS of work facing, pick up and K130[140:140] sts evenly around armhole edge. Work 2cm (¾in) in K1, P1 rib. Cast off evenly in rib.

TO MAKE UP

Press on WS of work using a warm iron over a damp cloth. Join side and armband seams. Press seams. Sew on buttons.

Design No. 5

CHILD'S SWEATER

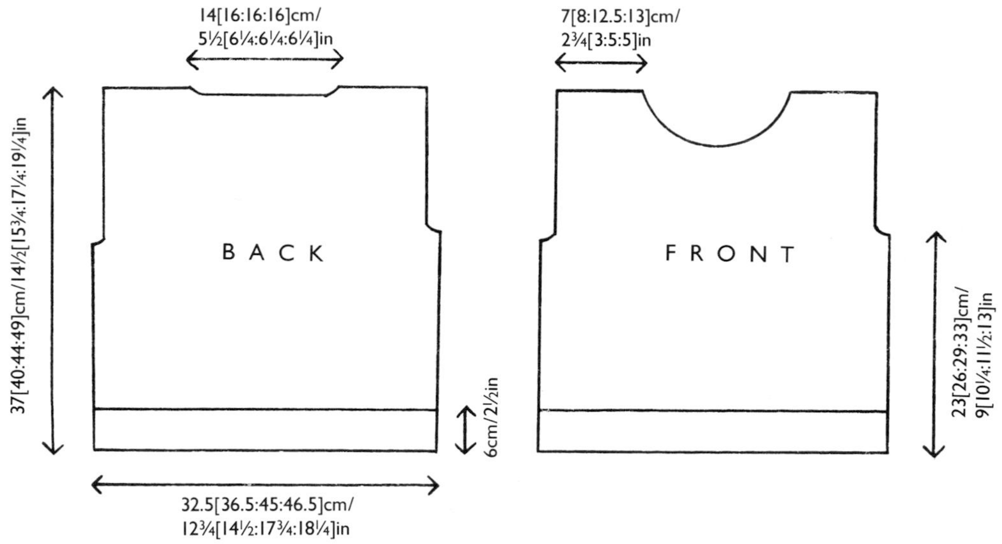
14[16:16:16]cm/
5½[6¼:6¼:6¼]in
7[8:12.5:13]cm/
2¾[3:5:5]in
37[40:44:49]cm/14½[15¾:17¼:19¼]in
BACK
FRONT
23[26:29:33]cm/
9[10¼:11½:13]in
6cm/2½in
32.5[36.5:45:46.5]cm/
12¾[14½:17¾:18¼]in

CHILD'S CARDIGAN

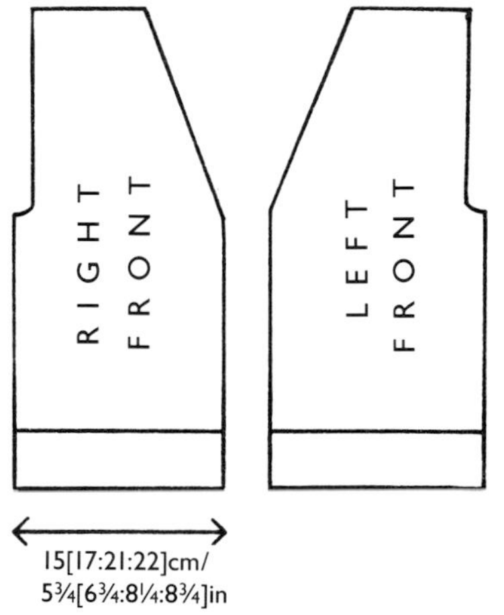
RIGHT FRONT
LEFT FRONT
15[17:21:22]cm/
5¾[6¾:8¼:8¾]in

ADULT'S SWEATER

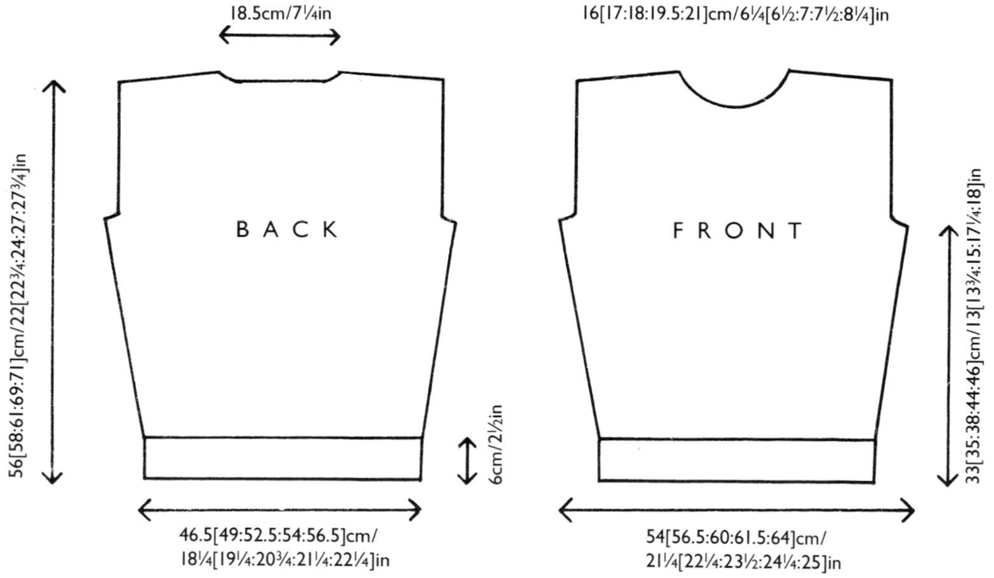
18.5cm/7¼in
16[17:18:19.5:21]cm/6¼[6½:7:7½:8¼]in
56[58:61:69:71]cm/22[22¾:24:27:27¾]in
BACK
FRONT
33[35:38:44:46]cm/13[13¾:15:17¼:18]in
6cm/2½in
46.5[49:52.5:54:56.5]cm/
18¼[19¼:20¾:21¼:22¼]in
54[56.5:60:61.5:64]cm/
21¼[22¼:23½:24¼:25]in

ADULT'S CARDIGAN

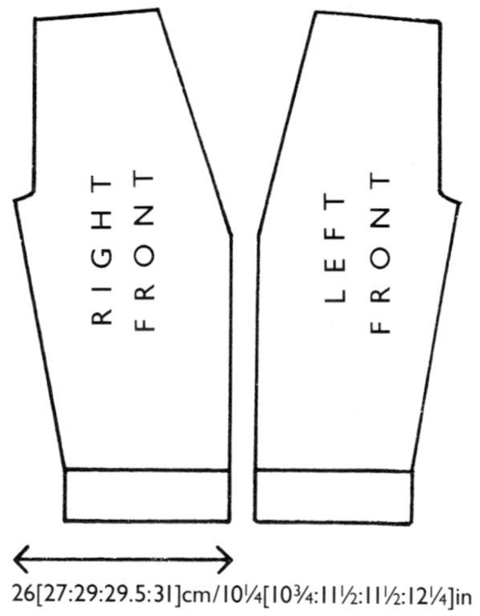
RIGHT FRONT
LEFT FRONT
26[27:29:29.5:31]cm/10¼[10¾:11½:11½:12¼]in

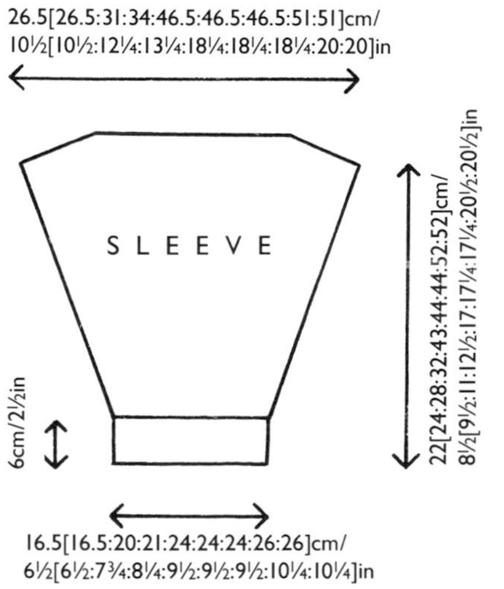
26.5[26.5:31:34:46.5:46.5:46.5:51:51]cm/
10½[10½:12¼:13¼:18¼:18¼:18¼:20:20]in
SLEEVE
22[24:28:32:43:44:44:52:52]cm/
8½[9½:11:12½:17:17¼:17¼:20½:20½]in
6cm/2½in
16.5[16.5:20:21:24:24:24:26:26]cm/
6½[6½:7¾:8¼:9½:9½:9½:10¼:10¼]in

ADULT'S WAISTCOAT

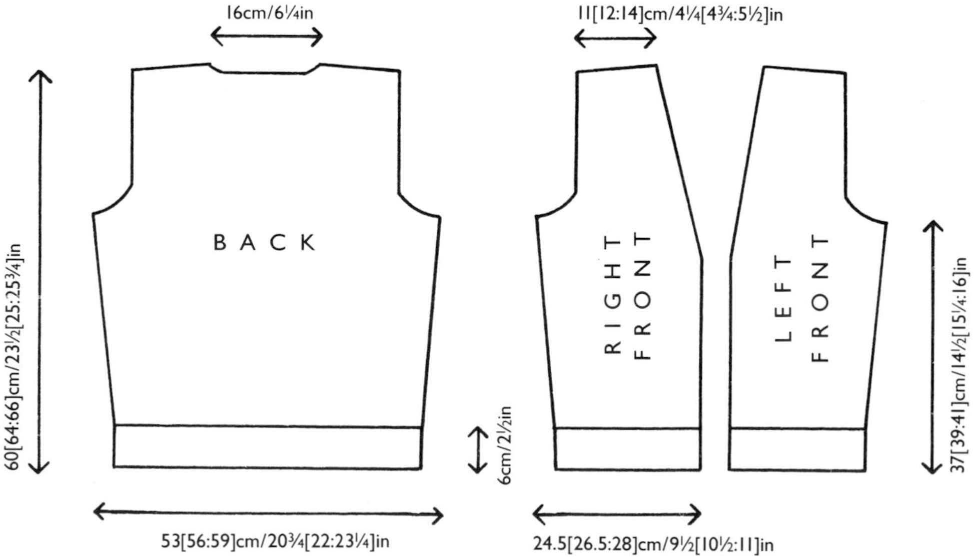
16cm/6¼in
11[12:14]cm/4¼[4¾:5½]in
60[64:66]cm/23½[25:25¾]in
BACK
RIGHT FRONT
LEFT FRONT
6cm/2½in
37[39:41]cm/14½[15¼:16]in
53[56:59]cm/20¾[22:23¼]in
24.5[26.5:28]cm/9½[10½:11]in

Design N°6

ALEXANDER
Rose

*A combination of rich, jewel colours
and the luxury of pure wool makes
a classic, but stunning, man's floral
patterned sweater.*

SIZES

To fit chest 107[112:117]cm (42[44:46]in)
Actual size 114[121:126]cm (45[47½:49½]in)
Length to shoulder 72.5[74.5:77.5]cm
(28½[29¼:30½]in)
Sleeve seam 55[55:57]cm (21½[21½:22½]in)
Figures in square brackets [ ] refer to larger
sizes; where there is only one set of figures, it
applies to all sizes

MATERIALS

8[9:9] × 50g balls of Rowan Designer DK in
main colour A (plum 657)
2 balls in each of 5 colours, B (tan 627), C
(buff 616), D (gold 650), E (dusty pink 70),
F (cherry 651)
1 ball in each of 6 colours, G (mauve 652),
H (air force 65), I (olive 639), J (pale green
664), K (sky 665), L (stone 656)
Pair each of 3¼mm (US3) and 4mm (US6)
knitting needles

TENSION

24½sts and 28 rows to 10cm (4in) over
intarsia patt using 4mm (US6) needles

BACK

Using 3¼mm (US3) needles and A, cast on
100 [106:110] sts.
1st row (K1 tb1, P1) to end.
Rep this row to form twisted rib for 6cm
(2½in), ending with a RS row.
Next row Rib 8[6:4], inc in next st. (rib 3,
inc in next st) to last 7[7:5] sts, rib to end.
122[130:136] sts.
Change to 4mm (US6) needles.

Beg with a K row, cont in st st and patt from
Chart, starting at row 15[9:1]. Read odd-
numbered (K) rows from right to left and
even-numbered (P) rows from left to right.
Strand colour not in use loosely across WS of
work where appropriate or use small, separate
balls of yarn for individual motifs.
Patt 10[12:12] rows. Inc one st at each end of
next and every foll 10th[12th:12th] row until
there are 140[148:154] sts. Cont without
shaping until Chart row 122 has been
completed, so ending with a P row.

Shape armholes

Cast off 3 sts at beg of next 2 rows, 2 sts at
beg of foll 2 rows and one st at beg of next 2
rows. 128[136:142] sts.*

Cont without shaping until Chart row 200
has been completed, so ending with a P row.

Shape shoulders and back neck

Next row Cast off 21[23:25] sts, patt until
there are 21[23:24] sts on right-hand needle,
turn.
Work one row. Cast off rem 21[23:24] sts.
With RS of work facing, s1 centre 44 sts on to
a holder, rejoin yarn to next st and patt to end.
Next row Cast off 21[23:25] sts, patt to end.
Work one row. Cast off rem 21[23:24] sts.

FRONT

Work as given for Back to *
Cont without shaping until Chart row 178 has
been completed, so ending with a P row.

*Disproving the belief that a floral
sweater is unsuitable for a man, Mark,
wearing 'Alexander Rose', relaxes against
the wood pile.*

Design Nº 6

A
B
C
D
E
F
G
H
I
J
K
L

191
181
171
161
151
141
131
121
111
101
91
81
71
61
51
41
31
21
11
1

SLEEVE
1ST SIZE BACK
2ND SIZE BACK
3RD SIZE BACK

34

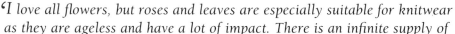
Shape neck

Next row Patt 55[59:62] sts, turn and leave rem sts on a spare needle.
Complete left side of neck first.
Cast off at beg of next and foll alt rows 4 sts once, 3 sts once, 2 sts once and one st 4 times. 42[46:49] sts. Cont without shaping until Chart row 200 (row 201 for other side of neck) has been completed, so ending at armhole edge.

Shape shoulder

Cast off 21[23:25] sts at beg of next row.
Work one row. Cast off rem 21[23:24] sts.
With RS of work facing, sl centre 18 sts on to a holder, rejoin yarn to next st and patt to end. Work one row, then complete as given for other side of neck, noting the bracketed exception.

SLEEVES

Using 3¼mm (US3) needles and A, cast on 50 sts. Work 6cm (2½in) in twisted rib as given for Back welt, ending with a RS row.
Next row Rib 2, (inc in next st, rib 3) to end. 62 sts.
Change to 4mm (US6) needles.
Beg with a K row, cont in st st and patt from Chart, inc one st at each end of 4th and every foll 3rd row until there are 102 sts, then at each end of every foll 4th row until there are 122 sts.
Cont without shaping until Chart row 138 [138:142] has been completed, so ending with a P row.

Shape top

Cast off 10 sts at beg of next 2 rows, 4 sts at beg of foll 12 rows and 8 sts at beg of next 2 rows. Cast off rem 38 sts.

'I love all flowers, but roses and leaves are especially suitable for knitwear as they are ageless and have a lot of impact. There is an infinite supply of references for roses. These roses are my favourite; they come from a nineteenth-century embroidered Russian rug. It was also a challenge for me to design a floral sweater for a man. This one has worked out well with the inclusion of leaves and using richer colourings rather than the traditional pastel shades.'

NECKBAND

Join right shoulder seam
Using 3¼mm (US3) needles, A and with RS of work facing, pick up and K21 sts down left front neck, K across 18 sts on holder, pick up and K21 sts up right front neck, one st down right back neck, K across 44 sts on holder and pick up and K one st up left back neck. 106 sts.
Work 9cm (3½in) in twisted rib. Cast off loosely in rib.

TO MAKE UP

Press on WS using a warm iron over a damp cloth. Join left shoulder and neckband seam. Fold neckband in half to inside and slip stitch in position. Set in sleeves. Join side and sleeve seams. Press seams.

The colours and patterns of 'Alexander Rose' harmonize with the woodland foliage.

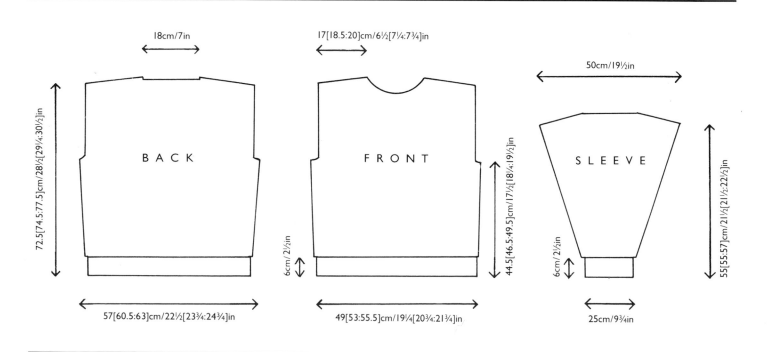

Design N.º 7

Necta

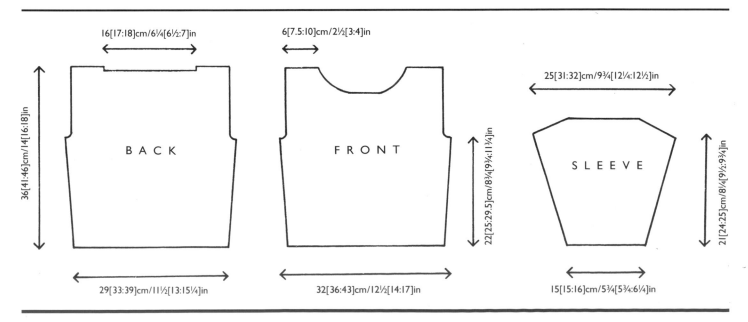

A stocking stitch, tunic-style sweater for a child with a striking intarsia pattern. Knitted in Rowan DK Cotton, the lower edge is decorated with multi-coloured tassels and the cuffs with crochet spheres.

SIZES

To fit chest 56[61-66:71-76]cm (22[24-26:28-30]in)
Actual size 64[72:86]cm (25 [28¼:34]in)
Length to shoulder 36[41:46]cm (14[16:18]in)
Sleeve seam 21[24:25]cm (8¼[9½:9¾]in)
Figures in square brackets [] refer to larger sizes; where there is only one set of figures, it applies to all sizes

MATERIALS

6[7:7] × 50g balls of Rowan DK Cotton in main colour A (China 267)
1 ball in each of 9 colours, B (Sunflower 261), C (Cherry 298), D (Scarlet 255), E (Kingfisher 273), F (Azure 248), G (Flame 254), H (Royal 294), I (Purple 272), J (True Navy 244)
Pair each of 3¼mm (US3) and 4mm (US6) knitting needles
3.50mm (US E/4) crochet hook

TENSION

20 sts and 28 rows to 10cm (4in) over intarsia patt using 4mm (US6) needles

BACK

Using 4mm (US6) needles and A, cast on 58[66:78] sts. Beg with a K row, cont in st st and patt from Chart, starting at row 25[11:1]. Read odd-numbered (K) rows from right to left and even-numbered (P) rows from left to right. Strand colour not in use loosely across WS of work where appropriate or use small, separate balls of yarn for individual motifs. Work 12[10:10]rows. Inc one st at each end of next and every foll 10th row until there are 64[72:86] sts. Cont without shaping until Chart row 86[82:82] has been completed, ending with a P row.

Shape armholes

Cast off 2[2:3] sts at beg of next 2 rows and 2 sts at beg of foll 2 rows. 56[64:76] sts. * Cont without shaping until Chart row 124[124:126] has been completed, ending with a P row.

Shape shoulders and back neck

Next row Patt 12[15:20], turn.
Work one row. Cast off these 12[15:20] sts. With RS of work facing, sl centre 32[34:36] sts on to a holder, rejoin yarn to next st and patt to end. Work 2 rows. Cast off rem 12[15:20] sts.

FRONT

Work as given for Back to *.
Cont without shaping until Chart row 112 has been completed, ending with a P row.

Shape neck

Next row Patt 20[24:30] sts, turn and leave rem sts on a spare needle.
Complete left side of neck first.
Cast off at beg of next and foll alt rows 4 sts

BACK

36[41:46]cm/14[16:18]in

16[17:18]cm/6¼[6½:7]in

29[33:39]cm/11½[13:15¼]in

FRONT

6[7.5:10]cm/2½[3:4]in

22[25:29.5]cm/8¾[9¾:11¾]in

32[36:43]cm/12½[14:17]in

SLEEVE

25[31:32]cm/9¾[12¼:12½]in

21[24:25]cm/8¼[9½:9¾]in

15[15:16]cm/5¾[5¾:6¼]in

Design Nº7

A
B
C
D
E
F
G
H
I
J

121

111

101

91

81

71

61

51

41

31

21

11

1

1ST SIZE BACK

2ND SIZE BACK

3RD SIZE BACK

Design N.º 7

once, 3 sts once and one st once [twice:3 times]. 12[15:20] sts. Cont without shaping until Chart row 126[126:128] has been completed, ending with a P row. (Work one more row for other side of neck). Cast off. With RS of work facing, sl centre 16 sts on to a holder, rejoin yarn to next st and patt to end. Work one row, then complete as given for other side of neck, noting the bracketed exception.

SLEEVES

Using 4mm (US6) needles and A, cast on 30[30:32] sts. Beg with a K row, cont in st st and patt from Chart, inc one st at each end of 4th and every foll 3rd row until there are 50[62:64] sts. Cont without shaping until Chart row 58[68:70] has been completed, ending with a P row.

Shape top

Cast off 4[3:4] sts at beg of next 2 rows, 3 sts at beg of foll 4 rows and 5[7:7] sts at beg of next 2 rows. Cast off rem 20[30:30] sts.

NECKBAND

Join right shoulder seam.
Using 3¼mm (US3) needles, A and with RS of work facing, pick up and K16[17:19] sts down left front neck, K across 16 sts on holder, pick up and K16[17:19] sts up right front neck, one st down right back neck, K across 32[34:36] back neck sts on holder and pick up and K one st up left back neck. 82[86:92] sts.
Work 5 rows in K1, P1 rib. Cast off evenly in rib.

TASSELS

(Make approximately 20 in a combination of all colours for around lower edge. Make approximately 4 balls in all colours for cuff edges.)

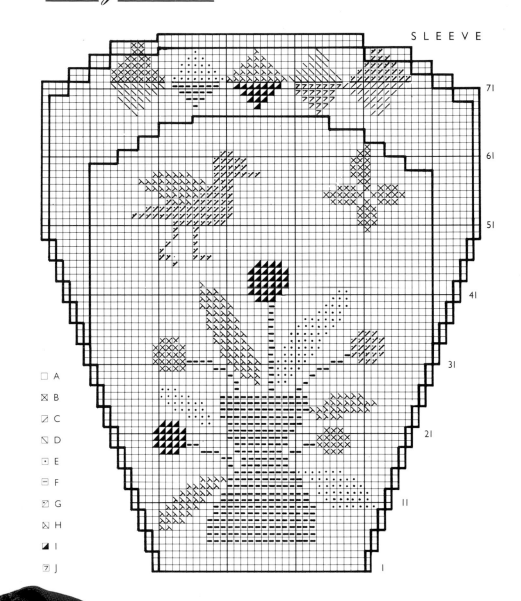

SLEEVE

- □ A
- ⊠ B
- ☑ C
- ◩ D
- ⊡ E
- ⊟ F
- ◪ G
- ◩ H
- ◤ I
- ◳ J

71
61
51
41
31
21
11
I

Ball
Using 3.50mm (US E/4) crochet hook make 2 ch.
1st round Work 8 dc into 2nd ch from hook.
2nd round Work 2 dc into each dc to end. 16dc.
3rd round (Miss 1dc, 1dc into next dc) to end. 8dc.
Cut off yarn, leaving a long end. Thread cut end through each of 8 sts and leave to pull up tight later for lower edge (pull up tight and fasten off if making ball section only for cuff edges).

Fringe
Cut 6 × 28cm (11in) lengths of yarn. Insert crochet hook through centre of ball and draw fringe (folded in half) through. Use end of yarn from working initial ch to sew end of fringe in position inside ball. At the opposite end, draw up thread to close ball and fasten off.

TO MAKE UP

Press on WS using a warm iron over a damp cloth. Join left shoulder and neckband seams. Set in sleeves. Join side and sleeve seams. Press seams. Sew tassels to lower edge and balls to cuff edge.

Design N°8

RUSSIAN
Wedding

This generous-sized cardigan is knitted in stocking stitch in an Aran-weight yarn. The intarsia pattern of wedding figures with floral borders and decoration appears to have been embroidered on to the fabric.

SIZES

To fit bust 87-96[102-112]cm (34-38[40-44]in)
Actual size 132[136]cm (52[53½]in)
Length to shoulder 69[75.5]cm (27[29¾]in)
Sleeve seam 37.5cm (14¾in)
Figures in square brackets [] refer to larger size; where there is only one set of figures, it applies to both sizes.

MATERIALS

9[9] × 100g hanks of Rowan Magpie Aran in main colour A (Natural 002 or Admiral 504)
3[4] × 50g balls of Rowan Designer DK in colour B (red 640)
1[2] balls of Designer DK in colour C (yellow 648)
2[2] balls of Designer DK in colour D (purple 99)
1[1] ball of Designer DK in colour E (navy 628 or tan 627)
1[1] ball of Designer DK in colour F (green 655)
1[2] balls of Designer DK in colour G (aqua 89)

2[2] balls of Designer DK in colour H (black 62 or stone 656)
Pair each of 4mm (US6) and 5mm (US8) knitting needles
8 buttons

TENSION

20 sts and 22 rows to 10cm (4in) over patt using 5mm (US8) needles

NOTE

All colours in Designer DK (B – H) are used double throughout the pattern.

The wedding motifs appear on the back of the cardigan as well as the fronts. The colours used here are typical of Russian embroideries, but the navy background could easily be replaced with black or ecru for an alternative colourway.

BACK

Using 4mm (US6) needles and A, cast on 102 sts.
1st row (WS) P2, (K2, P2) to end.
2nd row K2, (P2, K2) to end.
These 2 rows form the rib. Work 2 rows more.
Next row P7[1], inc in next st, (P2, inc in next st) to last 7[1] sts, P7[1]. 132[136] sts.
Change to 5mm (US8) needles.
Beg with a K row, cont in st st and work 1 row E, 2 rows B, 1 row G, 6 rows B, 1 row A, 1 row B.
Next row (K1 B, 1 A) to end.
Next row (P1 B, 1 A) to end.
Next row (K1 B, 1 A) to end.
Next row Using B, P to end.
These 16 rows form border patt.
Cont in patt from Chart, starting at row 11[1]. Read odd-numbered (K) rows from right to left and even-numbered (P) rows from left to right. Strand colour not in use loosely across WS of work where appropriate or use small, separate balls of yarn for individual motifs. Work until Chart row 88[92] has been completed.

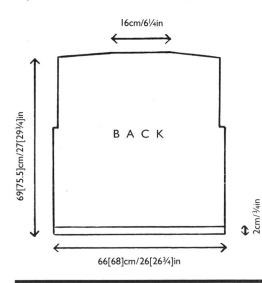

16cm/6¼in

69[75.5]cm/27[29¾]in

BACK

66[68]cm/26[26¾]in

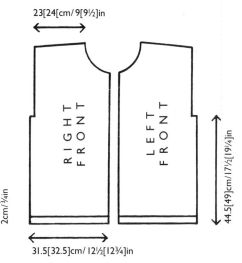

23[24[cm/ 9[9½]in

RIGHT FRONT

LEFT FRONT

2cm/¾in

44.5[49]cm/17½[19¼]in

31.5[32.5]cm/ 12½[12¾]in

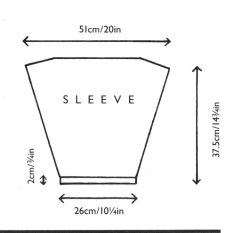

51cm/20in

SLEEVE

2cm/¾in

37.5cm/14¾in

26cm/10¼in

Design Nº 8

A
B
C
D
E
F
G
H

141
131
121
111
101
91
81
71
61
51
41
31
21
11
1

IST SIZE RIGHT FRONT

IST SIZE LEFT FRONT

IST SIZE BACK

2ND SIZE RIGHT FRONT

2ND SIZE LEFT FRONT

2ND SIZE BACK

'Walking into Rizzoli's book shop in New York I saw the most amazing
book on Russian embroidery. The illustrations gave me many ideas for
designs including this marriage ceremony with the bridal couple and their
bridesmaids.'

Shape armholes

Cast off 4 sts at beg of next 2 rows. 124[128] sts. Cont without shaping until Chart row 142[146] has been completed, so ending with a P row.

Shape shoulders and back neck

Next row Cast off 23[24] sts, patt until there are 23[24] sts on right-hand needle, turn and complete right side of neck first.
Work one row.
Cast off rem sts.
With RS of work facing, sl centre 32 sts on to a holder, rejoin yarn to next st and patt to end.
Next row Cast off 23[24] sts, patt to end. Work one row. Cast off rem 23[24] sts.

LEFT FRONT

Using 4mm (US6) needles and A, cast on 48 sts. Work 4 rows in K2, P2 rib.
Next row P2[8], inc in next st, (P2[1], inc in next st) to last 3[7] sts, P3[7]. 63[65] sts.
Change to 5mm (US8) needles.
Beg with a K row, cont in st st and work 12 rows border patt as given for Back.
Next row K1 B, (1 A, 1 B) to end.
Next row P1 A, (1 B, 1 A) to end.
Next row K1 B, (1 A, 1 B) to end.
Next row Using B, P to end.
Cont in patt from Chart, starting at row 11[1], until Chart row 88[92] (row 89[93] for Right Front) has been completed, so ending at side edge.

Shape armhole

Cast off 4 sts at beg of next row. 59[61] sts. Cont without shaping until Chart row 127[131] (row 128[132] for Right Front) has been completed, so ending at front edge.

Shape neck

Cast off at beg of next and foll alt rows 6 sts once, 3 sts twice and one st twice. 46[48] sts. Cont without shaping until Chart row 142[146] (row 143[147] for Right Front) has been completed, so ending at armhole edge.

Shape shoulder

Cast off 23[24] sts at beg of next row. Work one row. Cast off rem 23[24] sts.

RIGHT FRONT

Work as given for Left Front, noting the bracketed exceptions.

SLEEVES

Using 4mm (US6) needles and A, cast on 44 sts. Work 4 rows in K2, P2 rib.
Next row P4, (inc in next st, P4) to end. 52 sts.
Change to 5mm (US8) needles.
Beg with a K row, cont in st st and patt from Chart. Inc one st at each end of 3rd and every foll alt row until there are 64 sts, then at each end of foll 3rd row until 55th row of Chart has been completed.
Cont in A only, inc as before, until there are 102 sts. Cont without shaping until sleeve measures 37.5cm (14¾in) from beg, ending with a P row.

SLEEVE

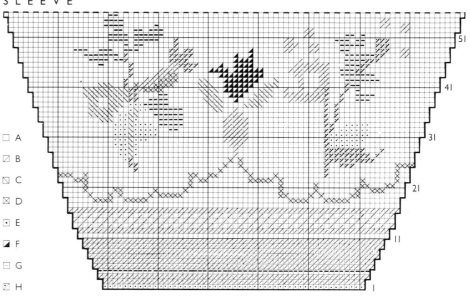

A
B
C
D
E
F
G
H

Shape top

Cast off 6 sts at beg of next 8 rows. Cast off rem 54 sts.

BUTTON BAND

Using 4mm (US6) needles and A, cast on 5 sts.
1st row K1, (P1, K1) twice.
Rep this row to form moss st until band, when slightly stretched, fits up Left Front to start of neck shaping, ending at inner edge. Cut off yarn. Leave sts on a safety-pin. Sew band in position.
Mark position for 7 buttons with pins. The first to come 3cm (1¼in) above lower edge, the last 14cm (5½in) down from neck with the others evenly spaced between.

BUTTONHOLE BAND

Work as given for Button Band, but do not cut off yarn and making buttonholes as markers are reached as foll:
Buttonhole row K1, P1, yo, K2 tog, K1. Sew band in position.

NECKBAND

Join shoulder seams.
Using 4mm (US6) needles, A and with RS of work facing, patt across sts of buttonhole band, pick up and K24 sts up right front neck, 2 sts down right back neck, K across 32 back neck sts on holder, pick up and K2 sts up left back neck, 24 sts down left front neck, then patt across 5 sts of button band. 94 sts.
Beg with a 1st row, work 3 rows in K2, P2 rib as given for Back.
Next row (buttonhole row) K2, yo, P2 tog, rib to end.
Cont in rib until neckband measures 3cm (1¼in) from beg. Cast off evenly in rib.

TO MAKE UP

Press on WS using a warm iron over a damp cloth. Sew sleeve tops in position all around armholes including cast-off sts at underarms. Join side and sleeve seams. Press seams. Sew on buttons.

Design N⁰ 9

Happy COAT

A charming child's jacket with distinctive two-colour borders that are reminiscent of their Chinese origins. The pattern consists of various pretty animal and flower motifs, according to the size of the garment. Embroidered flowers have been scattered on to the fabric at a later stage.

SIZES

To fit chest 56-61[61-66:66-71:76-81]cm (22-24[24-26:26-28:30-32]in)
Actual size 73.5[82:89.5:102]cm (28½[32¼:35¼:40]in)
Length to shoulder 37[40.5:44.5:50.5]cm (14½[16:17½:19¾]in)
Sleeve seam 20[24.5:30:34.5]cm (7¾[9½:11¾:13½]in)
Figures in square brackets [] refer to larger sizes; where there is only one set of figures, it applies to all sizes.

MATERIALS

4[5:6:7] × 50g balls of Rowan Designer DK in main colour A (navy 628)
1[2:2:3] balls in colour B (red 640)
1[2:2:2] balls in colour C (ecru 649)
Small amount of colour D (yellow 675) for embroidery only
Pair each of 3¼mm (US3) and 4mm (US6) knitting needles
6[6:7:7] toggle-style buttons

TENSION

22 sts and 30 rows to 10cm (4in) over st st using 4mm (US6) needles

BACK

Using 3¼mm (US3) needles and A, cast on 78[88:98:110] sts. Cont in moss st.
1st row (K1, P1) to end.
2nd row (P1, K1) to end.
Rep these 2 rows once more.
Change to 4mm (US6) needles.
Beg with a K row, cont in st st and work 18 rows in border patt from Chart A. Read odd-numbered rows from right to left and even-numbered rows from left to right. Strand

colour not in use loosely across WS of work. Cont in A only, work 46[50:58:72] rows, so ending with a P row.

Shape armholes

Cast off 2[2:3:3] sts at beg of next 2 rows and 2 sts at beg of foll 2 rows. 70[80:88:100] sts. Cont without shaping, work a further 40[46:50:54] rows, so ending with a P row.

Shape shoulders and back neck

Next row Cast off 10[12:13:16] sts, K until there are 9[11:13:16] sts on right-hand needle, turn.
Work one row. Cast of rem 9[11:13:16] sts.

With RS of work facing, sl centre 32[34:36:36] sts on to a holder, rejoin yarn to next st and K to end.
Next row Cast off 10[12:13:16] sts, P to end.
Work one row. Cast off rem 9[11:13:16] sts.

Frances explores the country lanes in dappled sunlight wearing her jacket that combines simple knitted stitches with embroidery.

44

Design Nº 9

'Brighton abounds with second-hand book shops tucked away in the Lanes and neighbouring back streets. On one of my frequent visits to these shops I found a book on Chinese peasant blue and white cross stitch work. Some of the elements from the book have been incorporated into this jacket for a child.'

CHART A

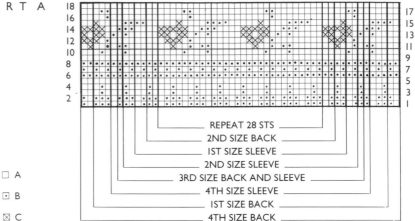

REPEAT 28 STS
2ND SIZE BACK
1ST SIZE SLEEVE
2ND SIZE SLEEVE
3RD SIZE BACK AND SLEEVE
4TH SIZE SLEEVE
1ST SIZE BACK
4TH SIZE BACK

□ A
⊡ B
⊠ C

LEFT FRONT

Using 3¼mm (US3) needles and A, cast on 44[50:52:60] sts. Work 4 rows moss st as given for Back welt, inc one st at side edge of last row for 1st, 3rd and 4th sizes. 45[50:53:61] sts.
Change to 4mm (US6) needles.
Beg with a K row, cont in st st and work 18 rows in border patt shown at lower edge of Chart for Left Front, *at the same time* keeping 2 sts in moss st at front edge throughout.
When border patt has been completed, cont in patt from main Chart, starting at row 41[31:19:1].
(Note that motif at lower corner of Chart is worked for 4th size only.)
Strand colour not in use loosely across WS of work where appropriate or use small, separate balls of yarn for individual motifs.
Cont in patt until Chart row 86[80:76:72] (row 87[81:77:73] for Right Front) has been completed, so ending at side edge.

Shape armhole

Cast off 2[2:3:3] sts at beg of next row and 2 sts at beg of foll alt row. 41[46:48:56] sts.
Cont without shaping until Chart row 121[121:119:119] (row 120[120:118:118] for Right Front) has been completed, so ending at front edge.

Shape neck

Cast off at beg of next and foll alt rows 11 sts once, 6 sts once, 4 sts once, 2 sts 0[1:0:1] time and one st 1[0:1:1] time. 19[23:26:32] sts. Cont without shaping until Chart row 130 (row 131 for Right Front) has been completed, so ending at armhole edge.

Shape shoulder

Cast off 10[12:13:16] sts at beg of next row. Work one row. Cast off rem 9[11:13:16] sts.

RIGHT FRONT

Work as given for Left Front (using the appropriate Chart), noting the bracketed exceptions.

SLEEVES

Using 3¼mm (US3) needles and A, cast on 36[40:42:44] sts. Work 4 rows in moss st. Change to 4mm (US6) needles.
Beg with a K row, cont in st st and work 18 rows in border patt from Chart A, *at the same time* inc one st at each end of 4th and every foll 3rd row. When border patt has been completed, cont in A only, inc as before, until there are 66[76:86:94] sts. Cont without shaping until sleeve measures 20[24.5:30:34.5]cm (7¾[9½:11¾:13½]in) from beg, ending with a P row.

Shape top

Cast off 8 sts at beg of next 2 rows, 4 sts at beg of foll 4[4:8:8] rows and 10 sts at beg of next 2 rows.
Cast off rem 14[24:18:26] sts.

NECKBAND

Join shoulder seams.
Using 3¼mm (US3) needles, A and with RS of work facing, pick up and K25[26:27:27] sts up right front neck, one st down right back neck, K across 32[34:36:36] sts on holder, pick up and K one st up left back neck and 25[26:27:27] sts down left front neck. 84[88:92:92] sts.
P one row and K one row.
Next row Using B, P to end.
Next row (K1 B, 1 A) to end.
Next row Using B, P to end.
Using A, work 2 rows in moss st.
Cast off.

TO MAKE UP

Press on WS of work using a warm iron over a damp cloth. Using D, embroider flowers as shown at random over back, fronts and sleeves. Set in sleeves. Join side and sleeve seams. Press seams. Sew on buttons to inner edge of front border. Embroider button loops in A on opposite edge.

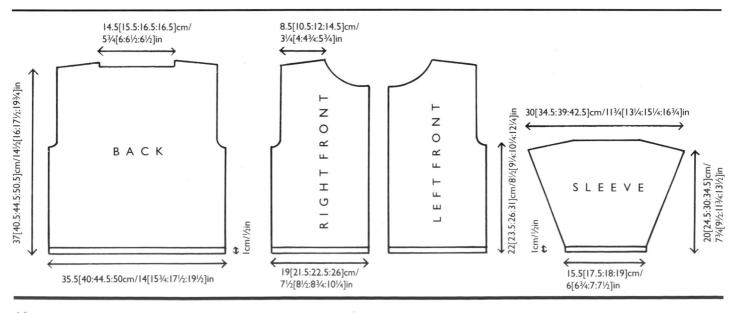

14.5[15.5:16.5:16.5]cm/
5¾[6:6½:6½]in

BACK

37[40.5:44.5:50.5]cm/14¼[16:17½:19¾]in

35.5[40:44.5:50cm/14[15¾:17½:19½]in

1cm/½in

8.5[10.5:12:14.5]cm/
3¼[4:4¾:5¾]in

RIGHT FRONT

LEFT FRONT

22[23.5:26:31]cm/8½[9¼:10¼:12¼]in

1cm/½in

19[21.5:22.5:26]cm/
7½[8½:8¾:10¼]in

30[34.5:39:42.5]cm/11¾[13¼:15¼:16¾]in

SLEEVE

20[24.5:30:34.5]cm/
7¾[9½:11¾:13½]in

1cm/½in

15.5[17.5:18:19]cm/
6[6¾:7:7½]in

Design N.º 9

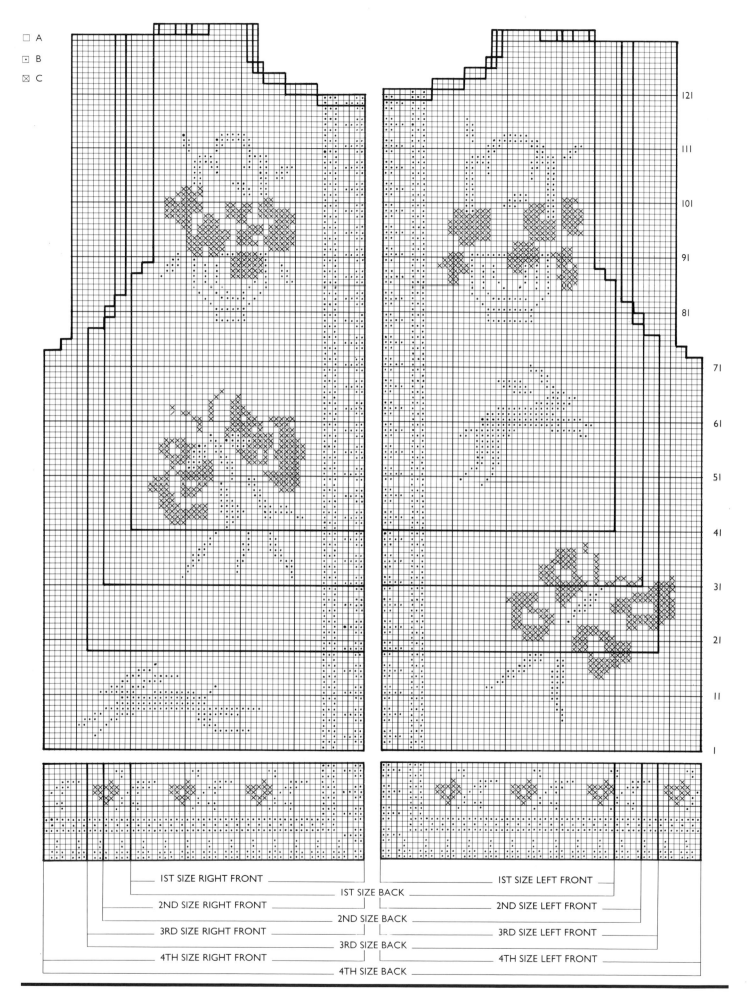

Denim

These are two easy-to-knit jackets in stocking stitch with moss stitch borders and Rowan's special denim yarn. The beadwork, based on American Indian slippers, is all optional – the jackets can be left plain or you can have fun creating your own beaded designs.

DENIM JACKET

SIZES

To fit bust/chest 81-87[91-96:102-107]cm (32-34[36-38:40-42]in)
Actual size 116[123:128]cm (45½[48½:50]in)
Length to shoulder 44[46.5:49]cm (17¼[18¼:19¼]in)
Sleeve seam (ladies') 37[37.5:37.5]cm (14½[14¾:14¾]in)
Sleeve seam (men's) 45[46.5:46.5]cm (17¾[18¼:18¼]in)
Figures in square brackets [] refer to larger sizes; where there is only one set of figures, it applies to all sizes

MATERIALS

16[17:18] × 50g balls of Rowan Den-m-nit DK in shade 230 (Tennessee)
Pair each of 3¾mm (US5) and 4mm (US6) knitting needles.
5 buttons
240 silver beads from a selection at suppliers (see page 143) if required.

TENSION

24 sts and 31 rows to 10cm (4in) over st st using 4mm (US6) needles after washing (see To Make Up).

LEFT FRONT

Using 4mm (US6) needles cast on 38[44:44] sts.
1st row (RS) K2, * (K1, P1) twice, K2, rep from * to end.

2nd row P2, * (P1, K1) twice, P2, rep from * to end.
These two rows form moss st and rib patt.
Rep them 7 times more, then work 1st row again.
Next row P4[14:6], inc in next st, (P6[14:7], inc in next st) to last 5[14:5] sts, P to end.
43[46:49] sts. **
Next row (RS) K3[4:7], P2, K26, P2, K10[12:12].
Next row P to end.
Rep last 2 rows to form main patt. Shape side edge by inc one st at beg (for Right Front, read 'end' here) of next row and at same edge on foll 4th and 3rd row alternately 17[18:18] times in all, *at the same time* when work measures 25[28:31]cm (9¾[11:12¼]in) from beg, ending with a RS row (end with a WS row here for Right Front), cont as foll:

Shape front edge

Dec one st at beg of next and every foll 6th row 12 times in all, *at the same time* when side edge shaping has been completed, work

1[3:7] rows straight, ending with a WS row (work one more row here for Right Front).

Shape armhole

Cont to shape at front edge as before, cast off 3 sts at beg of next row, 2 sts at beg of foll alt row and one st at beg of next alt row.
Keeping armhole edge straight, cont to dec at front edge only until work measures 43[46:49]cm (17[18:19¼]in) from beg, ending with a WS row. Cast off for yoke.
Cast on same number of sts as you have just cast off and cont in st st, keeping continuity of front edge shaping, until 42[46:49] sts rem.
Cont without shaping until work measures 12cm (4¾in) from beg, ending at armhole edge.

Shape shoulder

Cast off 21[23:25] sts at beg of next row.
Work one row. Cast off rem 21[23:24] sts.
Sew two pieces of Front tog with seam on RS of work to form yoke.

Denim jackets, with pockets and shaped collars, make perfect casual wear for Monica and Thomas. Silver stud beads have been used to highlight the features and pattern the yoke of Monica's jacket.

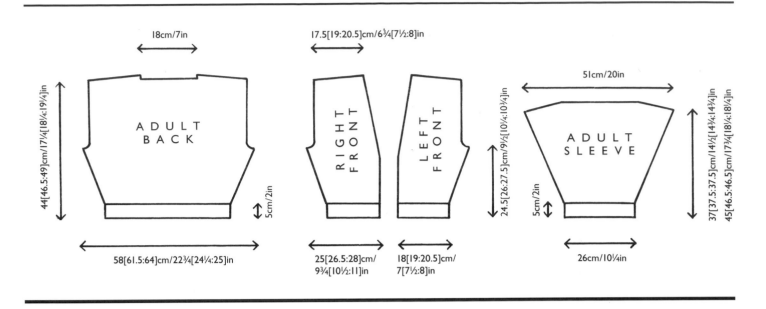

18cm/7in

17.5[19:20.5]cm/6¾[7½:8]in

51cm/20in

ADULT BACK

RIGHT FRONT

LEFT FRONT

ADULT SLEEVE

44[46.5:49]cm/17¼[18¼:19¼]in

24.5[26:27.5]cm/9½[10¼:10¾]in

37[37.5:37.5]cm/14½[14¾:14¾]in

45[46.5:46.5]cm/17¾[18¼:18¼]in

5cm/2in

5cm/2in

58[61.5:64]cm/22¾[24¼:25]in

25[26.5:28]cm/9¾[10½:11]in

18[19:20.5]cm/7[7½:8]in

26cm/10¼in

RIGHT FRONT

Work as given for Left Front to **.
Next row K10[12:12], P2, K26, P2, K3[4:7].
Next row P to end.
Cont in main patt, as set, as given for Left Front, noting the bracketed exceptions.

BACK

Using 4mm (US6) needles cast on 98[104:110] sts. Work 17 rows in moss st and rib patt as given for Left Front welt, ending with a RS row.
Next row P6[6:9], inc in next st, (P11[12:12], inc in next st) to last 7[6:9] sts, P to end. 106[112:118] sts.
Beg with a K row, cont in st st, inc one st at each end of 3rd and every foll 4th and 3rd row alternately until there are 140[148:154] sts. Cont without shaping, work 1[3:7] rows, ending with a P row.

Shape armholes

Cast off 3 sts at beg of next 2 rows, 2 sts at beg of foll 2 rows and one st at beg of next 2 rows. 128[136:142] sts. Cont without shaping until work measures 43[46:49]cm (17[18:19¼]in) from beg, ending with a P row. Cast off for yoke.
Cast on 128[136:142] sts and cont in st st for a few rows. Sew two pieces of Back tog with seam on RS of work to form yoke. Cont without shaping until Back measures same as Front to shoulder, ending with a P row.

Shape shoulders and back neck

Next row Cast off 21[23:25] sts, K until there are 21[23:24] sts on right-hand needle, turn. Work one row. Cast off rem 21[23:24] sts. With RS of work facing, rejoin yarn to next st and cast off centre 44 sts, K to end.
Next row Cast off 21[23:25] sts, P to end. Work one row. Cast off rem 21[23:24] sts.

SLEEVES

Using 4mm (US6) needles cast on 56 sts. Work 17 rows in moss st and rib patt as given

for Left Front welt, ending with a RS row.
Next row P5, inc in next st, (P8, inc in next st) to last 5 sts, P5. 62 sts.
Beg with a K row, cont in st st, inc one st at each end of 4th row (for ladies') or 5th row (for men's) and every foll 3rd row (for ladies') or 4th row (for men's) until there are 122 sts. Cont without shaping until work measures 46[46:47]cm (18[18:18½]in) (for ladies') or 56[56:57]cm (22[22:22½]in) (for men's), ending with a P row.

Shape top

Cast off 9 sts at beg of next 2 rows, 4 sts at beg of foll 8 rows and 12 sts at beg of next 2 rows. Cast off rem 48 sts.

POCKET TOPS

(make 2)

Using 3¾mm (US5) needles cast on 30 sts.
1st row (RS) (K1, P1) to end.
2nd row (P1, K1) to end.
Rep these 2 rows to form moss st. Work 10 rows more, ending with a WS row.
Cast off.

POCKETS

(make 2)

Using 4mm (US6) needles cast on 2 sts.
1st row (RS) K1, P1.
2nd row P1, K1.
3rd row (P1, K1 into next st) twice. 4 sts.
4th row K1, (P1, K1) into next st, (K1, P1) into next st, K1. 6 sts.
5th row K1, P1, (K into front and back of next st) twice, P1, K1. 8 sts.
6th row K1, P1, P into front and back of next st, P2, P into front and back of next st, P1, K1. 10 sts.
Cont to work moss st border and increases as set by last 2 rows until there are 30 sts, ending with a WS row. Cont without shaping, work 26 rows. Work 2 rows in moss st. Cast off K-wise.
Slip stitch pockets in position on Fronts, using 'P' lines on Fronts as guides for pocket sides. Sew pocket top above.

BUTTON BAND AND COLLAR

Join shoulder seams.
Using 3¾mm (US5) needles cast on 20 sts.
1st row (RS) (K1, P1) to end.
2nd row (P1, K1) to end.
Rep these 2 rows to form moss st until band fits up right front edge to start of shaping, ending with a WS row. (For Buttonhole Band, end with a RS row here.) Mark position of buttons with pins – the first to come 2cm (¾in) above cast-on edge and the last 2cm (¾in) below top of work, with the others evenly spaced between.

Shape collar

Cont in moss st, inc one st at end of next and every foll 6th row until there are 26 sts. Work 3 rows, so ending at straight edge.
Next row Cast off 10 sts, patt to end.
Next row Patt to end, turn and cast on 10 sts.
Cont to inc as before until there are 32 sts, then cont without shaping until collar fits up right front edge to shoulder. Mark shoulder edge with a coloured marker. Work a further 11cm (4¼in), ending with a WS row. Cast off in patt.

BUTTONHOLE BAND AND COLLAR

Work as given for Button Band and Collar, noting the bracketed exception and *at the same time* make buttonholes as markers are reached as foll:
1st buttonhole row (RS) Patt 13 sts, cast off next 2 sts, patt to end.
2nd buttonhole row Patt to end, casting on 2 sts over those cast off in previous row.

TO MAKE UP

Machine wash separately the knitted pieces at 60-70°. Dry, then press on WS of work using a warm iron over a damp cloth. Set in sleeves. Join side and sleeve seams. Sew front bands and collar in position, matching shaped front edges and joining back seam. Press seams. Sew on buttons. Sew on beads if required.

Design Nº 10

CHILD'S DENIM JACKET

SIZES

To fit chest 51-56[56-61:71-76]cm (20-22[22-24:28-30]in)
Actual size 60[72:92]cm (23½[28:36]in)
Length to shoulder 34[40:49]cm (13¼[15¾:19¼]in)
Sleeve seam 15[18:24]cm (5¾[7:9½]in)
Figures in square brackets [] refer to larger sizes; where there is only one set of figures, it applies to all sizes

MATERIALS

7[8:9] × 50g balls of Rowan Den-m-nit DK Cotton in shade 230 (Tennessee)
Pair each of 3¾mm (US5) and 4mm (US6) knitting needles
4[4:5] buttons
Beads (see page 143 for suppliers) – about 50 Indian glass beads H, about 120 Japanese silver lined Magatama turquoise, about 80 Magatama white and about 70 silver beads

TENSION

24 sts and 31 rows to 10cm (4in) over st st using 4mm (US6) needles after washing (see To Make Up).

BACK

Using 4mm (US6) needles cast on 60[74:96] sts.
1st row (RS) K1, P1[K0:K1, P1], K2, * (K1, P1) twice, K2, rep from * to last 2[0:2] sts, K1, P1[K0:K1, P1].
2nd row P1, K1[K0:P1, K1], P2, * (P1, K1) twice, P2, rep from * to last 2[0:2] sts, P1, K1[K0:P1, K1].
These two rows form moss st and rib patt.
Rep them 6 times more, then work 1st row again.
Next row P to end, inc 4 sts evenly across row. 64[78:100] sts.
Beg with a K row, cont in st st and work from Chart, starting at row 47[29:1]. Read odd-numbered (K) rows from right to left and even-numbered (P) rows from left to right.
Work 8[10:10] rows. Inc one st at each end of next and every foll 8th[10th:10th] row until there are 72[86:110] sts. Cont without shaping until Chart row 96[90:84] has been completed, so ending with a P row.

Shape armholes

Cast off 3 sts at beg of next 2 rows and 2 sts at beg of foll 2 rows. 62[76:100] sts. Cont without shaping until Chart row 122[118:114] has been completed, so ending with a P row.
Cast off to form seam line.
Cast on same number of sts and cont from Chart until row 138 has been completed, so ending with a P row.

Shape shoulders and back neck

Next row K15[19:31], turn.
Work one row. Cast off rem 15[19:31] sts.
With RS of work facing, rejoin yarn to next st and cast off centre 32[38:38] sts, K to end.

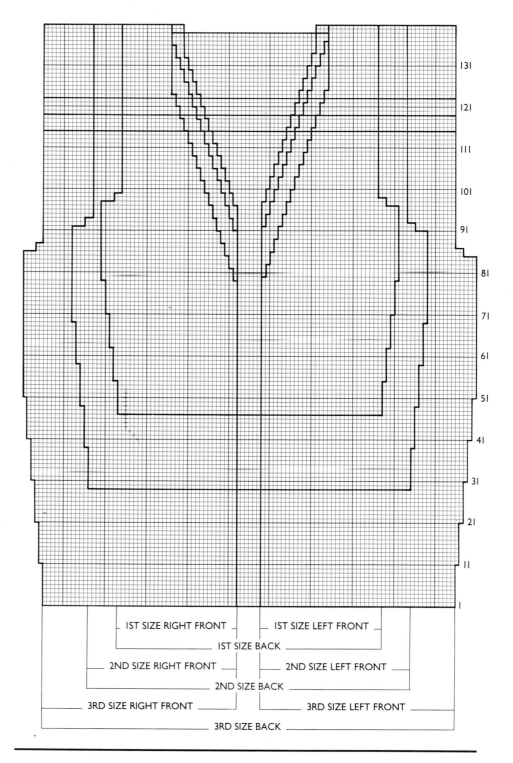

IST SIZE RIGHT FRONT — IST SIZE LEFT FRONT
IST SIZE BACK
2ND SIZE RIGHT FRONT — 2ND SIZE LEFT FRONT
2ND SIZE BACK
3RD SIZE RIGHT FRONT — 3RD SIZE LEFT FRONT
3RD SIZE BACK

'During my career I freelanced for a well-known manufacturer of denim jeans. It was an interesting job that took me all over the world.
The story of denim (the cloth) and indigo (the dye) is fascinating because of all the different processes that it goes through and the way in which the fabric lasts and lasts.
A few years ago I encouraged Rowan to launch an indigo-dyed cotton yarn that had a great response from the knitting public. I think it is very appropriate that our photographic location for this book was not far from Nîmes, the birthplace of denim or 'serge de Nîmes' as it was originally called.'

Work one row. Cast off rem 15[19:31] sts. Sew two pieces of Back tog with seam on RS of work to form yoke.

LEFT FRONT

Using 4mm (US6) needles cast on 26[34:44] sts.
1st row (RS) K2, * (K1, P1) twice, K2, rep from * to last 0[2:0] sts, K0[K1, P1:K0].
2nd row K0[P1, K1: K0], * P2, (P1, K1) twice, rep from * to last 2 sts, P2.
Rep these 2 rows 6 times more, then work 1st row again.
Next row P to end, inc 3[2:3] sts evenly across row. 29[36:47] sts.
Beg with a K row, cont in st st and work from Chart starting at row 47[29:1], shaping side edge, front edge and armhole as indicated.

RIGHT FRONT

Work as given for Left Front, but follow appropriate Chart.

SLEEVES

Using 4mm (US6) needles cast on 32[38:38] sts.
1st row (RS) K2, * (K1, P1) twice, K2, rep from * to end.
2nd row P2, * (P1, K1) twice, P2, rep from * to end.
Rep these 2 rows twice more. Beg with a K row, cont in st st, inc one st at each end of 3rd and every foll alt[alt:3rd] row until there are 52[58:84] sts.

1st and 2nd sizes only
Cont to inc at each end of every foll 3rd row until there are 64[74] sts.

All sizes
Cont without shaping until work measures 18[21.5:29]cm (7[8½:9½]in) from beg, ending with a P row.

Shape top
Cast off 6[7:8] sts at beg of next 2 rows, 3 sts at beg of foll 8 rows and 6[7:8] sts at beg of next 2 rows. Cast off rem 16[22:28] sts.

BUTTON BAND AND COLLAR

Join shoulder seams.
Using 3¾mm (US5) needles cast on 7 sts.
1st row (RS) K1, (P1, K1) to end.
Rep this row to form moss st until band fits up right front edge to start of shaping, ending with a WS row. (For Buttonhole Band, end with a RS row here.) Mark position of buttons with pins – the first to come 2cm (¾in) above cast-on edge and the last 2cm (¾in) below top of work with the others evenly spaced between.

Thomas loves his jacket in a proper denim yarn that matches his jeans. The studded yoke and collar, plus Indian-style beaded motifs, fit his 'tough guy' image of the Wild West in his favourite films.

Design Nº 10

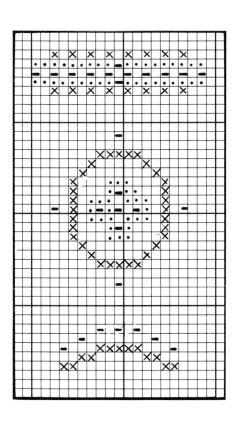

⊟ Indian glass bead

⊡ Japanese silver lined Magatama turquoise

☒ Magatama white

Shape collar

Cont in moss st, inc one st at end of next row and at same edge on every foll 3rd row until there are 17 sts. Work one row, so ending at straight edge.

Next row Cast off 5[6:6] sts, patt to end.

Next row Inc in first st, patt to end, turn and cast on 5[6:6] sts.

Cont to shape collar as before until there are 20[23:23] sts, then cont without shaping until collar fits up right front edge to shoulder. Mark shoulder edge with a coloured marker. Work a further 8[9.5:9.5]cm (3[3¾:3¾]in), ending with a WS row. Cast off in patt.

BUTTONHOLE BAND AND COLLAR

Work as given for Button Band and Collar, noting the bracketed exception and making buttonholes as markers are reached as foll:

Buttonhole row (RS) Patt 2, yo, K2 tog, patt 3.

POCKETS
(make 2)

Using 4mm (US6) needles cast on 28 sts. Work 4 rows in moss st. Beg with a K row, work 26 rows in st st, keeping 4 sts in moss st at each side. Work 4 more rows in moss st. Cast off.

TO MAKE UP

Machine wash the knitted pieces separately at 60-70°C. Dry, then press on WS of work using a warm iron over a damp cloth. Sew front bands and collar in position, matching shaped front edges and joining back seam. Sew on pockets as shown. Set in sleeves. Join side and sleeve seams. Press seams. Sew on buttons. Embroider bead motifs as shown on Chart.

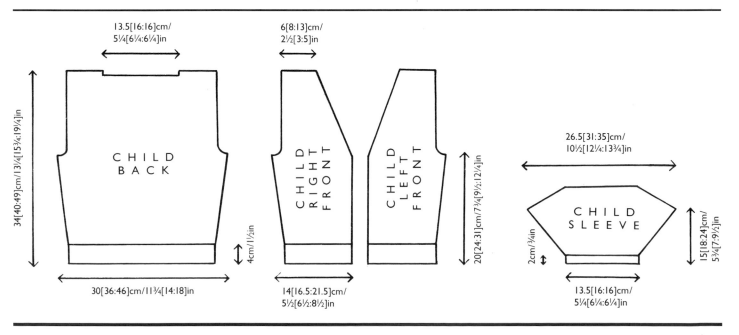

Design Nº 11

Elephant
TRAIL

This ladies' sweater is a loose shape for summer. It is knitted in a cool cotton yarn and the intarsia pattern has a strong Indian influence, including a deep border of elephant motifs. A knitted lace border trimmed with glass beads adds interest to the lower edge, neck and sleeves.

SIZES

To fit bust 87-92[97-102:107-112]cm (34-36[38-40:42-44]in)
Actual size 128[134:140]cm (50[53:55]in)
Length to shoulder 72.5[75.5:79]cm (28½[29¾:31]in)
Sleeve seam 46.5[49:51]cm (18¼[19¼:20]in)
Figures in square brackets [] refer to larger sizes; where there is only one set of figures, it applies to all sizes

MATERIALS

15[15:16] × 50g balls of Rowan Handknit DK Cotton in main colour A (Pimpernel 249)
3[4:4] balls in colour B (Clover 266)
2[3:3] balls in colour C (Mustard 246)
3[3:4] balls in colour D (Ecru 251)
4[4:4] balls in colour E (China 267)
Pair of 4mm (US6) knitting needles
Approximately 63 glass drop beads

TENSION

20 sts and 24½ rows to 10cm (4in) over intarsia patt using 4mm (US6) needles

BACK

Using 4mm (US6) needles and A, cast on 15 sts for lace border. K one row. Cont in patt from Lace Border Chart (see page 59), reading odd-numbered (RS) rows from right to left and even-numbered (WS) rows from left to right. Rep the 44 rows of patt 4 times in all shaping lower edge as shown, by dec one st at beg of 1st row, then inc one st at beg of 11 foll alt rows, then dec one st at beg of next 10 alt rows. Cast off 15 sts.
Using 4mm (US6) needles, A and with RS of work facing, pick up and K128[134:140] sts along top edge of lace border. P one row. Beg with a K row, cont in st st and patt from Chart, starting at row 17[9:1]. Read odd-numbered (K) rows from right to left and even-numbered (P) rows from left to right. Strand colour not in use loosely across WS of work or use small, separate balls of yarn for individual motifs. Cont in patt until Chart row 96 has been completed, so ending with a P row.

Shape armholes

Cast off 3 sts at beg of next 2 rows, 2 sts at beg of foll 2 rows and one st at beg of next 2 rows. 116[122:128] sts. *
Cont without shaping until Chart row 164 has been completed, so ending with a P row.

Togetherness is wearing eye-catching sweaters with a matching theme – elephants – in colours and patterns that clash and blend together successfully to make Eastern magic. Tijan is in 'Elephant Trail' with its pretty jewelled lace hem while Frances wears 'Nellie' (see page 59).

Design Nº 11

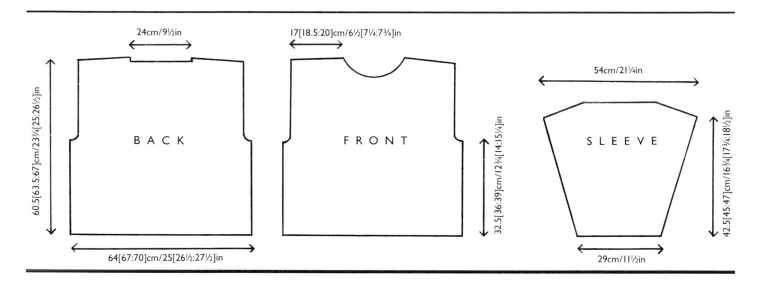

Shape shoulders and neck
Next row Cast off 18[19:20] sts, K until there are 16[18:20] sts on right-hand needle, turn.
Work one row. Cast off rem 16[18:20] sts.
With RS of work facing, rejoin yarn to next st and cast off centre 48 sts, K to end.
Next row Cast off 18[19:20] sts, P to end.
Work one row. Cast off rem 16[18:20] sts.

FRONT

Work as given for Back to *
Cont without shaping to Chart row 150, so ending with a P row.

Shape neck
Next row Patt 48[51:54] sts, turn and leave rem sts on a spare needle.
Complete left side of neck first. Cast off at beg of next and foll alt rows 6 sts once, 4 sts once, 2 sts once and one st twice. 34[37:40] sts. Cont without shaping to Chart row 164 (row 165 for other side of neck), so ending at armhole edge.

Shape shoulder
Cast off 18[19:20] sts at beg of next row.
Work one row. Cast off rem 16[18:20] sts.
With RS of work facing, rejoin yarn to next st and cast off centre 20 sts, patt to end. Work one row, then complete as given for other side of neck, noting the bracketed exception.

SLEEVES

Using 4mm (US6) needles and A, cast on 8 sts. K one row. Commence cuff patt.
1st row (WS) P1, K2, yo, sl next 2 sts K-wise, one at a time, then insert the tip of the left-hand needle into the fronts of these sts from the left and K them tog – called ssk, K1, (yo)

Reflecting on an Indian summer, Tijan looks pensive in her long loose sweater that is cool and comfortable to wear especially as it is knitted in a cotton yarn. There is no restrictive ribbing at the neck or cuff edges.

twice, K1, (yo) twice, K1.
2nd row (K1, K1 then P1 into yo twice of previous row) twice, K2, P1, K3.
3rd row P1, K2, yo, ssk, K7.
4th row Cast off 4 sts, K4 including st used to cast off, P1, K3.

Rep these 4 rows to form patt. Cont in patt until cuff measures 26cm (10¼in) from beg, ending with a 4th row. Cast off.
Using 4mm (US6) needles, A and with RS of work facing, pick up and K58 sts along top edge of cuff. P one row. Beg with a K row, cont in st st and patt from Chart, inc one st at each end of 4th and every foll 3rd row until there are 108 sts. Cont without shaping until Chart row 104[110:116] has been completed, so ending with a P row.

Shape top
Cast off 8 sts at beg of next 2 rows, 4 sts at beg of foll 10 rows and 10 sts at beg of next 2 rows. Cast off rem 32 sts.

COLLAR

Join shoulder seams.
Using 4mm (US6) needles and A, cast on 5 sts. K one row. Commence patt.
1st row (WS) P1, K2, (yo) twice, K1, (yo) twice, K1.
2nd row (K1, K1 then P1 into yo twice of previous row) twice, K3.
3rd row P1, K8.
4th row Cast off 4 sts, K to end.
Rep these 4 rows to form patt.
Cont in patt until collar fits all round neck edge, ending with a 4th row. Cast off.

TO MAKE UP

Press on WS of work using a warm iron over a damp cloth. Sew collar to neck edge, joining ends at left shoulder seam. Set in sleeves. Join side and sleeve seams. Press seams. Sew 5 beads on to each point of lace border below bobbles. Sew rem beads to centre of flower motifs and on to elephants as shown.

Nellie

The girl's version of the 'Elephant Trail' sweater echoes the same loose shape and knitted lace borders. The pattern mainly concentrates on the delightful band of colourful elephant motifs.

SIZES

To fit chest 56-61[66-71:76-81]cm (22-24[26-28:30-32]in)
Actual size 72[82:98]cm (28½[32¼:38½]in)
Length to shoulder 38[42:45.5]cm (15[16½:18]in)
Sleeve seam 21[26.5:30]cm (8¼[10¼:11¾]in)
Figures in square brackets [] refer to larger sizes; where there is only one set of figures, it applies to all sizes

MATERIALS

6[6:7] × 50g balls of Rowan DK Cotton in main colour A (China 267)
1 ball in each of 4 contrast colours, B (Mustard 246), C (Pimpernel 249), D (Ecru 251), E (Azure 248)
Pair of 4mm (US6) knitting needles

TENSION

20 sts and 28 rows to 10cm (4in) over st st using 4mm (US6) needles

NOTE

For 1st and 2nd sizes the lace border is worked in one piece for the Back and Front and sewn on later. For 3rd size the lace border is worked separately for the Back and Front, then the stitches for those sections are picked up from the border.

LACE BORDER

Using 4mm (US6) needles and A, cast on 15 sts. K one row. Cont in patt from Lace Border Chart, reading odd-numbered (RS) rows from right to left and even-numbered (WS) rows from left to right. Work 44 rows of patt 5[5:3] times in all, shaping lower edge as shown by dec one st at beg of 1st row, then inc one st at beg of 11 foll alt rows, then dec one st at beg of next 10 alt rows.
Cast off 15 sts.

BACK

1st and 2nd sizes only
Using 4mm (US6) needles and A, cast on 72[82] sts.
3rd size only
Using 4mm (US6) needles, A and with RS of work facing, pick up and K98 sts along top edge of border. P one row.

LACE BORDER CHART

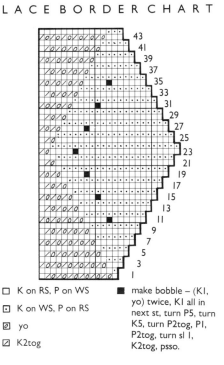

43
41
39
37
35
33
31
29
27
25
23
21
19
17
15
13
11
9
7
5
3
1

□ K on RS, P on WS
⊡ K on WS, P on RS
⊘ yo
⊠ K2tog

■ make bobble – (K1, yo) twice, K1 all in next st, turn P5, turn K5, turn P2tog, P1, P2tog, turn sl 1, K2tog, psso.

Frances wears a sweater that is influenced by the characters from her favourite bedtime stories. She is fascinated to hear about the adventures of Babar the elephant and other animals from the jungle.

All sizes

Beg with a K row, cont in st st and patt from Chart, starting at row 19[11:1]. Read odd-numbered (K) rows from right to left and even-numbered (P) rows from left to right. Strand colour not in use loosely across WS of work where appropriate or use small, separate balls of yarn for individual motifs. Cont in patt until Chart row 50 has been completed, so ending with a P row.

Shape armholes

Cast off 3 sts at beg of next 2 rows and 2 sts at beg of foll 2 rows. 62[72:88] sts. * Cont without shaping until Chart row 88[92:92] has been completed, so ending with a P row.

Shape shoulders and back neck

Next row Patt 16[19:26] sts, turn.
Work one row. Cast off these 16[19:26] sts. With RS of work facing, rejoin yarn to rem sts, cast off centre 30[34:36] sts, patt to end. Work 2 rows. Cast off rem 16[19:26] sts.

FRONT

Work as given for Back to *
Cont without shaping until Chart row 74[78:78] has been completed, so ending with a P row.

Shape neck

Next row Patt 26[29:37] sts, turn and leave rem sts on a spare needle.
Complete left side of neck first. Cast off at beg of next and foll alt rows 4 sts once, 3 sts once, 2 sts once and one st once[once:twice]. 16[19:26] sts. Cont without shaping until Chart row 90[94:94] has been completed, so ending with a P row. (Work one more row for other side of neck). Cast off.
With RS of work facing, rejoin yarn to rem sts, cast off centre 10[14:14] sts, patt to end. Work one row, then complete as given for other side of neck, noting the bracketed exception.

Design Nº 12

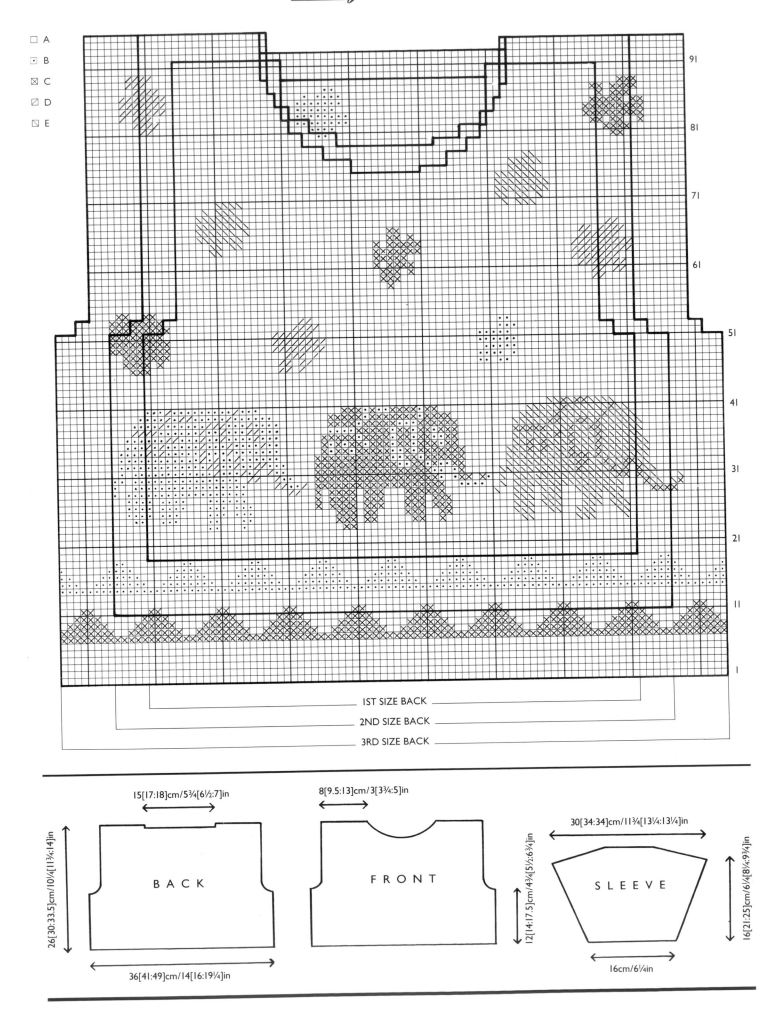

A
B
C
D
E

91
81
71
61
51
41
31
21
11
1

1ST SIZE BACK
2ND SIZE BACK
3RD SIZE BACK

15[17:18]cm/5¾[6½:7]in

8[9.5:13]cm/3[3¾:5]in

30[34:34]cm/11¾[13¼:13¼]in

26[30:33.5]cm/10¼[11¾:14]in

BACK

FRONT

SLEEVE

12[14:17.5]cm/4¾[5½:6¾]in

16[21:25]cm/6¼[8¼:9¾]in

36[41:49]cm/14[16:19¼]in

16cm/6¼in

'My family's background in India and the abundance of 'treasures' collected and brought back over the years have culminated in two related designs – 'Elephant Trail' for an adult and 'Nellie' for a child. Both garments are in the clear, bright colours that I associate with India and feature the ever popular elephant motif.'

SLEEVES

Using 4mm (US6) needles and A, cast on 8 sts for lace border. K one row.
1st row (WS) P1, K2, yfwd, ssk, (K1; yo twice), K1.
2nd row (K1, then K1 and P1 into yo twice of previous row) twice, K2, P1, K3.
3rd row P1, K2, yfwd, ssk, K7.
4th row Cast off 4 sts, K4 including st used to cast off, P1, K3.
Rep last 4 rows until border measures 14.5cm (5¾in) from beg, ending with a 4th row. Cast off.
Using 4mm (US6) needles, A and with RS of work facing, pick up and K32 sts along top edge of border. P one row. Beg with a K row, cont in st st and patt from Chart, inc one st at each end of 3rd[4th:4th] row and every foll alt[3rd:3rd] row until there are 60[68:68] sts. Cont without shaping until Chart row 44[58:70] has been completed, so ending with a P row.

Shape top
Cast off 4 sts at beg of next 2 rows, 3 sts at beg of foll 4[10:10] rows and 6 sts at beg of next 2[0:0] rows. Cast off rem 28[30:30] sts.

NECK BORDER

Join shoulder seams.
Using 4mm (US6) needles and A, cast on 5 sts. K one row.
1st row (WS) P1, K1, (K1, yo twice) twice, K1.
2nd row (K1, K1 then P1 into yo twice of previous row) twice, K3.
3rd row P1, K8.
4th row Cast off 4 sts, K to end.
Rep last 4 rows until border, slightly stretched, fits around neck edge, ending with a 4th row. Cast off.

TO MAKE UP

Press on WS using a warm iron over a damp cloth. Sew border to neck edge, joining ends at left shoulder seam. Set in sleeves. Join side and sleeve seams. For 1st and 2nd sizes only, join ends of Lace Border and sew to hem with seam at centre back of garment. Press seams.

SLEEVE

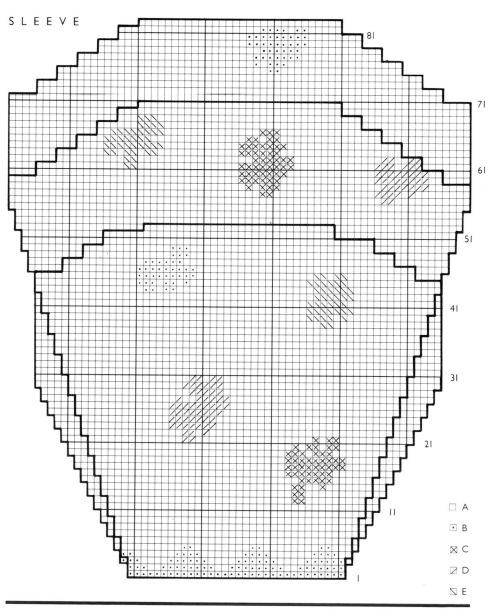

□ A
· B
⊠ C
⊡ D
⊠ E

Beads

Two easy-to-knit cotton sweaters decorated with beads. The child's sweater is in Rowan Soft Cotton with the beads incorporated into the delicate crochet edgings. For the woman's sweater in Rowan Mercerised Cotton shimmering beaded stripes are knitted into the fabric at regular intervals.

SIZES

Child's Sweater

To fit chest 51[56:61-66:71-76]cm (20[22:24-26:28-30]in)
Actual size 54[61:71:81]cm (21½[24:28:32]in)
Length to shoulder 25[31:39:45]cm (9¾[12¼:15¼:17¾]in)
Sleeve seam 20[26.5:31.5:36]cm (7¾[10½:12½:14]in)

Ladies' Sweater

To fit bust 87-91[91-96:96-102]cm (34-36[36-38:38-40]in)
Actual size 103[107:112]cm (40½[42:44]in)
Length to shoulder 52.5[54.5:56.5]cm (20¾[21½:22¼]in)
Sleeve seam 37[38:38]cm (14½[15:15]in)
Figures in square brackets [] refer to larger sizes; where there is only one set of figures, it applies to all sizes

MATERIALS

Child's Sweater

3[4:5:6] × 50g balls of Rowan Sea Breeze in Catmint 556
Beads (see page 143 for suppliers)
– glass rocailles 8/0, approx 198[220:245:260] in each of blue, turquoise and pink

Ladies' Sweater

10[10:11] × 50g balls of Rowan Cabled Mercerised Cotton in Black (319)
Beads (see page 143 for suppliers)
-rocailles 6/0, approx 530[550:570]g in black

Monica and petite Annabel (niece of the author) display their beaded sweaters against the velvet opulence of the chaise longue in their location château. Annabel's sweater is very simple to knit; it teams well with her pretty flower-sprigged skirt.

Pair each of 2¾mm (US2) and 3mm (US3) knitting needles
2.50mm (US B/1) crochet hook

NOTE

For Ladies' Sweater, thread beads on to a separate ball of yarn and use this to work bead rows.

TENSION

31 sts and 43 rows to 10cm (4in) over st st using 3mm (US3) needles

CHILD'S SWEATER

BACK

Using 2¾mm (US2) needles cast on 84[94:110:126] sts.
1st row (RS) (K1, P1) to end.
2nd row (P1, K1) to end.
Rep these 2 rows once more to form moss st border.
Change to 3mm (US3) needles.
Beg with a K row, cont in st st until work measures 12[17:24:29]cm (4¾[6½:9½:11½]in) from beg, ending with a P row.

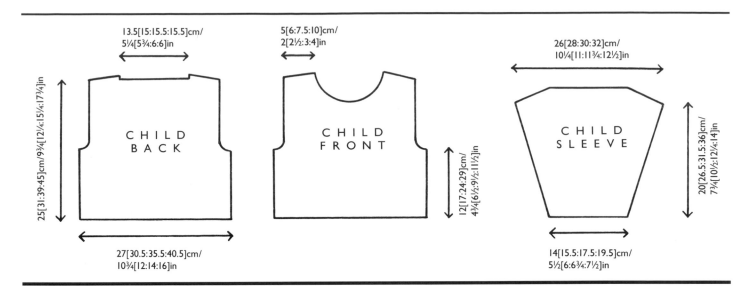

13.5[15:15.5:15.5]cm/
5¼[5¾:6:6]in

5[6:7.5:10]cm/
2[2½:3:4]in

26[28:30:32]cm/
10¼[11:11¾:12½]in

25[31:39:45]cm/9¾[12¼:15¼:17¾]in

27[30.5:35.5:40.5]cm/
10¾[12:14:16]in

C H I L D B A C K

C H I L D F R O N T

12[17:24:29]cm/
4¾[6½:9½:11½]in

C H I L D S L E E V E

20[26.5:31.5:36]cm/
7¾[10½:12¼:14]in

14[15.5:17.5:19.5]cm/
5½[6:6¾:7½]in

Shape armholes

Cast off 3[3:4:4] sts at beg of next 4 rows. 72[82:94:110] sts. Cont without shaping until work measures 25[31:39:45]cm (9¾[12¼:15¼:17¾]in) from beg, ending with a P row.

Shape shoulders and back neck

Next row K21[24:29:37], turn and complete right side of neck first.
Next row Cast off 4 sts, work to end.
Next row Cast off 8[9:12:16] sts, work to end.
Next row Cast off 2 sts, work to end.
Cast off rem 7[9:11:15] sts.
With RS of work facing, rejoin yarn to next st and cast off centre 30[34:36:36] sts, K to end. Work one row, then complete as given for other side of neck.

HEM BORDER

Thread beads on to yarn in foll sequence: 5 blue, 5 pink and 5 turquoise. Rep until there are 14[16:18:21] groups of 15 beads.

Using 2.50mm (US B/1) hook and with RS of work facing, join yarn to lower edge with a ss, * work 5ch, pull up 5 blue beads and ss into last ch worked, pull up 5 pink beads and ss into last ch worked, pull up 5 turquoise beads and ss into last ch worked – so forming a 3-colour cluster, 5ch, ss into hem of garment about 2cm (¾in) from previous ss, rep from * evenly across hem. Fasten off.

FRONT

Work as given for Back until work measures 20[26:34:40]cm (7¾[10¼:13¼:15¾]in) from beg, ending with a P row.

Shape neck

Next row K28[32:38:46], turn and leave rem sts on a spare needle.
Complete left side of neck first. Cast off at beg of next and foll alt rows 6 sts once, 3 sts once, 2 sts once and one st 2[3:4:4] times. 15[18:23:31] sts. Cont without shaping until Front measures same as Back to shoulder, ending at armhole edge.

Shape shoulder

Cast off 8[9:12:16] sts at beg of next row. Work one row. Cast off rem 7[9:11:15] sts. With RS of work facing, rejoin yarn to next st and cast off centre 16[18:18:18] sts, K to end. Work one row, then complete as given for other side of neck.

HEM BORDER

Work as given for Back.

SLEEVES

Using 2¾mm (US2) needles cast on 44[48:54:60] sts. Work 4 rows in moss st as given for Back border.
Change to 3mm (US3) needles.
Beg with a K row, cont in st st, inc one st at each end of 5th[5th:6th:7th] and every foll 4th[4th:5th:5th] row until there are 80[88:94:100] sts. Cont without shaping until Sleeve measures 20[26.5:31.5:36]cm (7¾[10½:12½:14]in) from beg, ending with a P row.

Shape top

Cast off 8 sts at beg of next 2 rows, 3 sts at beg of foll 8[8:12:10] rows and 8 sts at beg of next 2[2:2:4] rows. Cast off rem 24[32:26:22] sts.

NECKBAND

Join right shoulder seam.
Using 2¾mm (US2) needles and with RS of work facing, pick up and K60[60:62:62] sts evenly around front neck and 42[46:48:48] sts around back neck. 102[106:110:110] sts. Work 5 rows in moss st. Cast off in patt.

TO MAKE UP

Press on WS of work using a warm iron over a damp cloth. Join left shoulder and neckband seam. Set in sleeves. Join side and sleeve seams. Press seams.

NECK BORDER

Thread beads on to yarn in foll sequence: 1 blue, 1 pink, 1 turquoise. Rep until there are 29[30:31:31] groups of 3 beads.
Using 2.50mm (US B/1) hook and with RS of work facing, join yarn to left shoulder seam with a ss, * work 2ch, pull up 3 beads, ss into last ch worked to form a cluster, 2ch, ss into neckband about 1cm (½in) from previous ss, rep from * evenly around neckband. Join with a ss into same place as first ss. Fasten off.

CUFF BORDER

Work as given for Neck Border, making 14[15:17:19] bead clusters and starting and finishing at Sleeve seam.

LADIES' SWEATER

BACK

Using 3mm (US3) needles cast on 130[136:144] sts. Beg with a K row, cont in st st, inc one st at each end of 7th and every foll 6th row until there are 160[166:174] sts, *at the same time* work bead row on 13th and every foll 12th row as foll:
Bead row P1, P to last st working bead in front of every st, P last st.
Cont without shaping until work measures 28[30:32]cm (11[11¾:12½]in) from beg, ending with a WS row.

Shape armholes

Keeping bead patt correct, cast off 4 sts at beg of next 4 rows. 144[150:158] sts. Cont without shaping until work measures 51[53:55]cm (20[20¾:21½]in) from beg, ending with a WS row.

Monica looks stunning in her beaded sweater. Knitting with beads is easy, especially here where the background fabric is stocking stitch and the beads are added in simple stripes.

Design N.º 13

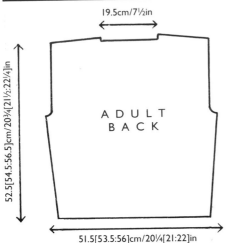

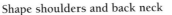

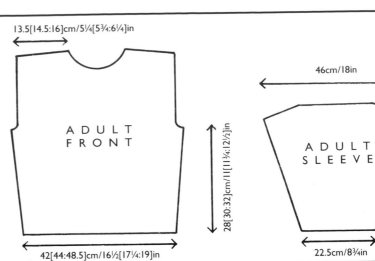

ADULT BACK — 19.5cm/7½in — 51.5[53.5:56]cm/20¼[21:22]in — 52.5[54.5:56.5]cm/20¾[21½:22¼]in

ADULT FRONT — 13.5[14.5:16]cm/5¼[5¾:6¼]in — 42[44:48.5]cm/16½[17¼:19]in — 28[30:32]cm/11[11¾:12½]in

ADULT SLEEVE — 46cm/18in — 22.5cm/8¾in — 37[38:38]cm/14½[15:15]in

---

'I have used beads in many of my collections. They are perfect for introducing a different element of surface decoration and I love choosing from the vast selection of beads that is available – their shapes, colours and textures are so exciting.

These sweaters, influenced by elegant evening wear from the 1940's, look very expensive, yet they are simple to make.'

Shape shoulders and back neck

Next row Patt 50[53:57] sts, turn and complete right side of neck first.
Next row Cast off 4 sts, patt to end.
Next row Patt to end.
Next row Cast off 2 sts, patt to end.
Rep last 2 rows once more.
Next row Cast off 21[23:25] sts, patt to end.
Next row Patt to end.
Cast off rem 21[22:24] sts.
With RS of work facing, rejoin yarn to next st and cast off centre 44 sts, patt to end. Work one row, then complete as given for other side of neck.

HEM BORDER

Work as given for Back of Child's Sweater, using black beads instead of colours and making 21[22:24] clusters along edge.

FRONT

Work as given for Back until work measures 46[48:50]cm (18[18¾:19½]in) from beg, ending with a WS row.

Shape neck

Next row K63[66:70], turn and leave rem sts on a spare needle.
Complete left side of neck first. Cast off at beg of next and foll alt rows 6 sts once, 4 sts once, 3 sts once, 2 sts 3 times and one st twice. 42[45:49] sts. Cont without shaping until Front matches Back to shoulder, ending at armhole edge.

Shape shoulder

Cast off 21[23:25] sts at beg of next row. Work one row. Cast off rem 21[22:24] sts.
With RS of work facing, rejoin yarn to next st and cast off centre 18 sts, K to end. Work one row, then complete as given for other side of neck.

HEM BORDER

Work as given for Back.

SLEEVES

Using 3mm (US3) needles cast on 70 sts. Beg with a K row, cont in st st and work bead row on 13th and every foll 12th row as before, *at the same time* inc one st at each end of 5th and every foll 4th row until there are 142 sts. Cont without shaping until Sleeve measures 37[38:38]cm (14½[15:15]in) from beg, ending with a WS row.

Shape top

Cast off 5 sts at beg of next 2 rows, 4 sts at beg of foll 12 rows and 8 sts at beg of next 2 rows. Cast off rem 68 sts.

NECKBAND

Join left shoulder seam.
Using 2¾mm (US2) needles and with RS of work facing, pick up and K74 sts evenly around front neck and 60 sts around back neck. 134 sts.
Work 3 rows in moss st. Cast off evenly in patt.

TO MAKE UP

Join right shoulder and neckband seam. Set in sleeves. Join side and sleeve seams. Work bead border around hem as given for Child's Sweater.

Carolean

Identical jackets knitted in a pure wool yarn and simple stocking stitch look totally different depending on the colours chosen – elegant in a plain ecru or young and bold in brighter colours. Unusual designer features include a beautiful deep lace border that forms the edgings and collar plus sculptured floral embroidery on the yoke with knitted bobbles and sewn leaves.

SIZES

To fit chest/bust 61[66-71:71-76:81-86:92-97:102-107]cm (24[26-28:28-30:32-34:36-38:40-42]in)
Actual size 76.5[87:96.5:105:116:127.5]cm (30[34¼:37¾:41½:45½:50]in)
Length to shoulder 48[51.5:55:61:64:67]cm (18¾[20¼:21½:24:25:26½]in)
Sleeve seam 28[33:37.5:48.5:50.5:52.5]cm (11[13:14¾:18¾:19¾:20¾]in)
Figures in square brackets [] refer to larger sizes; where there is only one set of figures, it applies to all sizes.

MATERIALS

Colourway 1 (Child's jacket)
7[8:9:13:14:15] × 50g balls of Rowan Designer DK in main colour A (jade 661)
1 ball in each of 4 colours, B (cherry 651), C (red 673), D (yellow 643) and E (chestnut 662)
Small amounts of F (navy 671) and G (cedar 665) for embroidery only

Colourway 2 (Ladies' jacket)
5[6:7:10:11:12] × 50g balls of Rowan Designer DK in main colour A (ecru 649)
2[2:3:3:4:4] × 50g balls of Rowan Cotton Glacè in colour B (Ecru 725)
Pair each of 3¼mm (US3) and 4mm (US6) knitting needles
4[4:5:5:6:6] buttons

TENSION

22 sts and 30 rows to 10cm (4in) over st st using 4mm (US6) needles

STITCH NOTE

Make a bobble as foll: (K1, yo, K1, yo, K1) all into same st to make 5 sts, turn and P5, turn and K5, turn and P2 tog, P1, P2 tog, turn and sl 1, K2 tog, psso

BACK

Using 4mm needles and A, cast on 80[92:102:104:116:128] sts. Beg with a K row, cont in st st.
4th, 5th and 6th sizes only
Inc one st at each end of 13th and every foll 12th row until there are 114[128:140] sts.

All sizes
Cont without shaping until work measures 25[27.5:30:24:27:30]cm (9¾[10¾:11¾:9½:10¾:11¾]in) from beg, ending with a P row.

Shape armholes
Cast off 3 sts at beg of next 2 rows, 2 sts at beg of foll 2 rows and 0[1:1:1:1:1] st at beg of next 2 rows. 70[80:90:102:116:128] sts. Cont without shaping until work measures 41[44.5:48:53:56:59]cm (16[17½:18¾:20¾:22:23¼]in) from beg, ending with a P row.

Shape shoulders and back neck
Next row K25[28:33:37:44:50], turn and leave rem sts on a spare needle.
Complete right side of neck first.

'White on white is always so understatedly chic. Here I have used it in many forms, from lace and stitchwork to embroidery – to make a stunning jacket. A creative knitter could easily extend the 'flower' pattern on the yoke by increasing the number of bobbles and adding extra embroidery. Or, as an alternative, how about experimenting with black on black? After the restrained elegance of the woman's jacket, I had fun using brighter colours for the child's version.'

Next row Cast off 2 sts, work to end.
Next row Work to end.
Next row Cast off 2 sts, work to end.
Cast off 11[12:15:17:20:23] sts at beg of next row. Work one row. Cast off rem 10[12:14:16:20:23] sts.
With RS of work facing, rejoin yarn to rem sts and cast off centre 20[24:24:28:28:28] sts, K to end. Work one row, then complete as given for other side of neck.

POCKET LININGS
(make 2)

Using 4mm (US6) needles and A, cast on 20[20:20:28:28:28] sts. Beg with a K row, work 28[28:28:38:38:38] rows in st st. Cut off yarn. Leave sts on a holder.

LEFT FRONT

Using 4mm (US6) needles and A, cast on 37[43:48:49:55:61] sts. Beg with a K row, cont in st st.

1st, 2nd and 3rd sizes only
Work 28 rows, so ending with a P row.
4th, 5th and 6th sizes only
Inc one st at beg (for Right Front, read 'end' here) of 13th and every foll 12th row until there are 52[58:64] sts. Work one row without shaping, so ending with a P row.

All sizes
Place pocket
Next row K5[7:10:6:10:14], sl next 20[20:20:28:28:28] sts on to a holder, K across sts of first pocket lining, K12[16:18:18:20:22].
4th, 5th and 6th sizes only
Cont in st st, inc at side edge as before until there are 54[61:67] sts.

All sizes
Cont without shaping until work measures 16[12:10:2:2:2] rows (for Right Front, read '17[13:11:3:3:3]' rows here) less than Back to underarm.

Cont in bobble patt from Chart, working shaping as indicated and reading odd-numbered (K) rows from right to left and even-numbered (P) rows from left to right.

RIGHT FRONT

Work as given for Left Front, noting the bracketed exceptions and reversing the position of the pocket.

SLEEVES

Using 4mm (US6) needles and A, cast on 38[40:42:58:58:58] sts. Beg with a K row, cont in st st, inc one st at each end of 3rd[5th:5th:3rd:3rd:3rd] and every foll 3rd[4th:4th:3rd:3rd:3rd] row until there are 68[72:78:126:126:126] sts. Cont without shaping until Sleeve measures 21[26:30.5:41.5:43.5:45.5]cm (8¼[10¼:12:16¼:17:18]in) from beg, ending with a P row.

Shape top
Cast off 5[6:6:12:12:12] sts at beg of next 2 rows, 4[3:3:6:6:6] sts at beg of foll 6[8:8:8:8:8] rows and 8[6:8:10:10:10] sts at beg of next 2 rows. Cast off rem 18[24:26:34:34:34] sts.

SLEEVE BORDER

Using 3¼mm (US3) needles and A (for Colourway 1) or B (for Colourway 2), cast on 10 sts. K one row. Cont in lace patt.
1st row Sl 1, K2, yo, K2 tog, * (yo) twice, K2 tog, (yo) twice, K2 tog, K1 *.
2nd row ** Sl 1, (K1, K1, P1 into yo twice of previous row) twice **, K2, yo, K2 tog, K1.
3rd row Sl 1, K2, yo, K2 tog, K2, rep from * to * as given for 1st row.
4th row Rep from ** to ** as given for 2nd row, K4, yo, K2 tog, K1.
5th row Sl 1, K2, yo, K2 tog, K4, rep from * to *.
6th row Rep from ** to **, K6, yo, K2 tog, K1.
7th row Sl 1, K2, yo, K2 tog, K6, rep from * to *.
8th row Rep from ** to **, K8, yo, K2 tog, K1.
9th row Sl 1, K2, yo, K2 tog, K8, rep from * to *.
10th row Rep from ** to **, K10, yo, K2 tog, K1.
11th row Sl 1, K2, yo, K2 tog, K15.

Design N.º 14

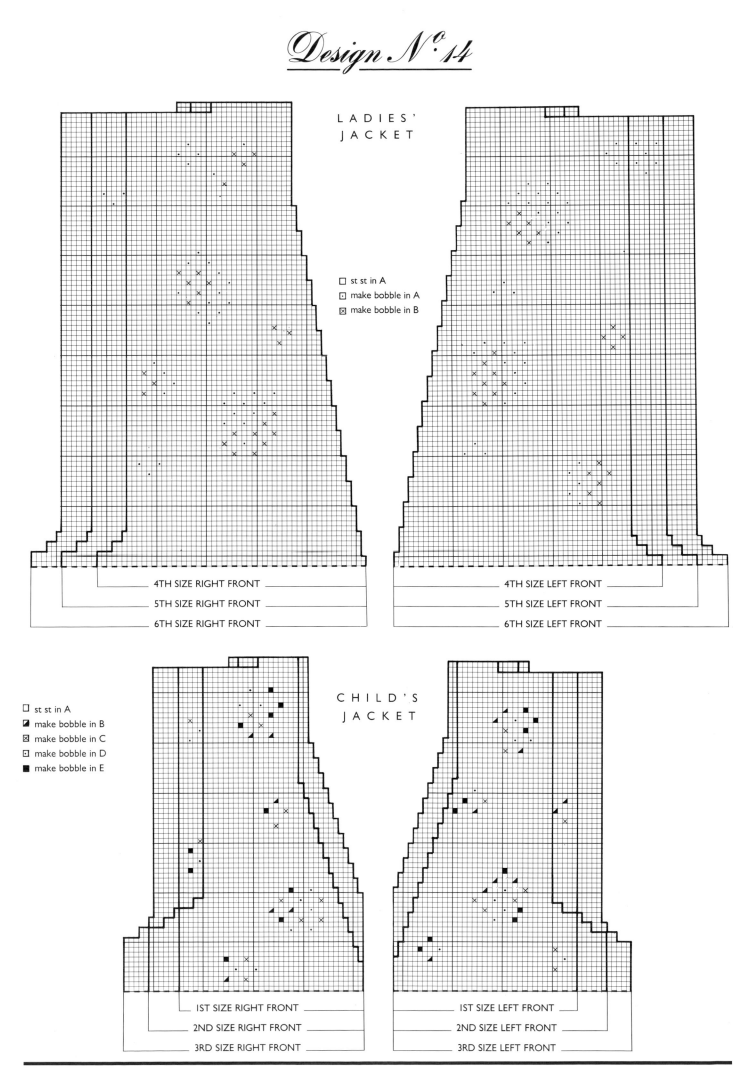

LADIES' JACKET

☐ st st in A
⊡ make bobble in A
⊠ make bobble in B

4TH SIZE RIGHT FRONT
5TH SIZE RIGHT FRONT
6TH SIZE RIGHT FRONT

4TH SIZE LEFT FRONT
5TH SIZE LEFT FRONT
6TH SIZE LEFT FRONT

CHILD'S JACKET

☐ st st in A
◪ make bobble in B
⊠ make bobble in C
⊡ make bobble in D
■ make bobble in E

1ST SIZE RIGHT FRONT
2ND SIZE RIGHT FRONT
3RD SIZE RIGHT FRONT

1ST SIZE LEFT FRONT
2ND SIZE LEFT FRONT
3RD SIZE LEFT FRONT

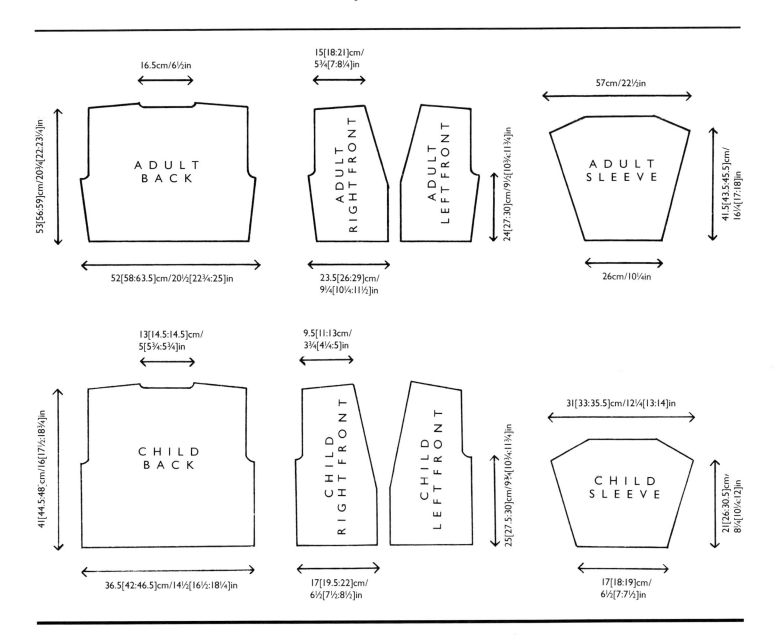

Adult Back: 16.5cm/6½in; 53[56:59]cm/20¾[22:23¼]in; 52[58:63.5]cm/20½[22¾:25]in

Adult Right Front / Adult Left Front: 15[18:21]cm/5¾[7:8¼]in; 24[27:30]cm/9½[10¾:11¾]in; 23.5[26:29]cm/9¼[10¼:11½]in

Adult Sleeve: 57cm/22½in; 41.5[43.5:45.5]cm/16¼[17:18]in; 26cm/10¼in

Child Back: 13[14.5:14.5]cm/5[5¾:5¾]in; 41[44.5:48]cm/16[17½:18¾]in; 36.5[42:46.5]cm/14½[16½:18¼]in

Child Right Front / Child Left Front: 9.5[11:13]cm/3¾[4¼:5]in; 25[27.5:30]cm/9¾[10¾:11¾]in; 17[19.5:22]cm/6½[7½:8½]in

Child Sleeve: 31[33:35.5]cm/12¼[13:14]in; 21[26:30.5]cm/8¼[10¼:12]in; 17[18:19]cm/6½[7:7½]in

12th row Cast off 10 sts, K7 including st used to cast off, yo, K2 tog, K1.
Rep rows 1-12 until border fits along cast-on edge of Sleeve, ending with a 12th row. Cast off.

POCKET TOPS

Using 4mm (US6) needles, A and with RS of work facing, K across 20[20:20:28:28:28] pocket sts on holder. Work 2cm (¾in) in K1, P1 rib. Cast off evenly in rib.

TO MAKE UP

Press on WS of work using a warm iron over a damp cloth. Slip stitch pocket linings in

place on WS of work and ends of pocket tops on RS. Using yarns F and G (for Colourway 1) or B (for Colourway 2), embroider leaves around bobbles as shown in photograph. Join shoulder and side seams.

MAIN BORDER

1st, 2nd and 3rd sizes only
Work as given for Sleeve border until 12 rows have been completed.
4th, 5th and 6th sizes only
Using 3¼mm (US3) needles and A (for Colourway 1) and B (for Colourway 2), cast on 14 sts. K one row. Cont in lace patt.
1st row Sl 1, K2, yo, K2 tog, K4, rep from * to * as given for Sleeve border.
2nd row Rep from ** to **, K6, yo, K2 tog, K1.
3rd row Sl 1, K2, yo, K2 tog, K6, rep from * to *.
4th row Rep from ** to **, K8, yo, K2 tog, K1.
5th row Sl 1, K2, yo, K2 tog, K8, rep from * to *.

6th row Rep from ** to **, K10, yo, K2 tog, K1.
7th row Sl 1, K2, yo, K2 tog, K10, rep from * to *.
8th row Rep from ** to **, K12, yo, K2 tog, K1.
9th row Sl 1, K2, yo, K2 tog, K12, rep from * to *.
10th row Rep from ** to **, K14, yo, K2 tog, K1.
11th row Sl 1, K2, yo, K2 tog, K19.
12th row Cast off 10 sts, K11 including st used to cast off, yo, K2 tog, K1.

All sizes
Rep rows 1-12 until border fits all round outer edge, ending with a 12th row and finishing at left side seam. Cast off. Sew border in position as you are working.
Sew sleeve border in position. Join sleeve seams. Set in sleeves. Press border and seams. Sew buttons on to left front border close to seam – the top one level with a 'yo' hole closest to start of neck shaping and the others evenly spaced opposite 'yo' holes down front.

Even in a rustic setting Pam looks classically elegant in this pretty jacket with its textured yoke. The embroidery on young Annabel's jacket echoes the colours in the flowers around her.

Design Nº 15

Natasha

Two very different colourways – one pastel and pretty, the other deep and jewel bright – make a special floral-patterned cardigan in mother and daughter sizes. The beaded yoke on the woman's cardigan is a labour of love well worth the stunning results, while the child's cardigan is lightly dotted all over with pale translucent beads.

SIZES

To fit chest/bust 56[61-66:71-76:81:87:91:96]cm (22[24-26:28-30:32:34:36:38]in)
Actual size 62.5[70.5:89:90.5:94:99:104]cm (24½[27¾:35:35½:37:39:41]in)
Length to shoulder 29[35.5:37.5:41:42:46:50]cm (11½[14:14¾:16:16½:18:19½]in)
Sleeve seam 23[25:29:33:46:47:48]cm (9[9¾:11½:13:18:18½:18¾]in)
Figures in square brackets [] refer to larger sizes; where there is only one set of figures, it applies to all sizes

MATERIALS

Colourway 1 (Ladies' Cardigan)
A = cherry 651, B = midnight blue 671, C = mauve 652, D = cedar 655, E = honey 675
Beads (see page 143 for suppliers)
– Japanese metallic rocailles 8/0, about 500 in gold; Japanese silver lined rocailles 8/0, about 350 each in royal and green plus about 400 in red; Japanese Ceylon pearlised 8/0, about 600 in white.

Colourway 2 (Child's cardigan)
A = pink 668, B = sky 665, C = lilac 666, D = sage 669, E = straw 643
4[5:6:7:8:9:10] × 50g balls of Rowan Designer DK in main shade A
1 ball in each of 4 shades, B, C, D and E
Beads (see page 143 for suppliers)
-Japanese Ceylon pearlised 8/0, about 250[300:350:400] in white

Pair each of 3¼mm (US3) and 4mm (US6) knitting needles
6[7:7:8:8:9:9] buttons

TENSION

24 sts and 30 rows to 10cm (4in) over intarsia patt using 4mm (US6) needles

BACK

Using 3¼mm (US3) needles and A, cast on 70[76:100:100:94:98:102] sts.
1st row (RS) (K1 tbl, P1) to end.
Rep this row to form twisted rib (or work in K1, P1 rib) for 7cm (2¾in), ending with a WS row.
Change to 4mm (US6) needles.
Beg with a K row, cont in st st and patt from Chart, starting at row 63[45:39:29:25:13:1]
Read odd-numbered (K) rows from right to left and even-numbered (P) rows from left to right. Strand colour not in use loosely across WS of work where appropriate or use small, separate balls of yarn for individual motifs. Work 6[6:8:10:3:4:4] rows. Inc one st at each end of next and every foll 6th[6th:8th:8th:3rd:4th:4th] row until there are 76[86:108:110:114:120:126] sts. Cont without shaping until Chart row 92[92:86:84:60:60:60] has been completed, so ending with a P row.

The colourways of these cardigans worn by Tijan and Frances are so different that it takes some time to realize that they are knitted from the same floral pattern. For anyone who is uncertain of knitting with beads, these jewels are sewn on separately after the garment has been completed.

Design Nº 15

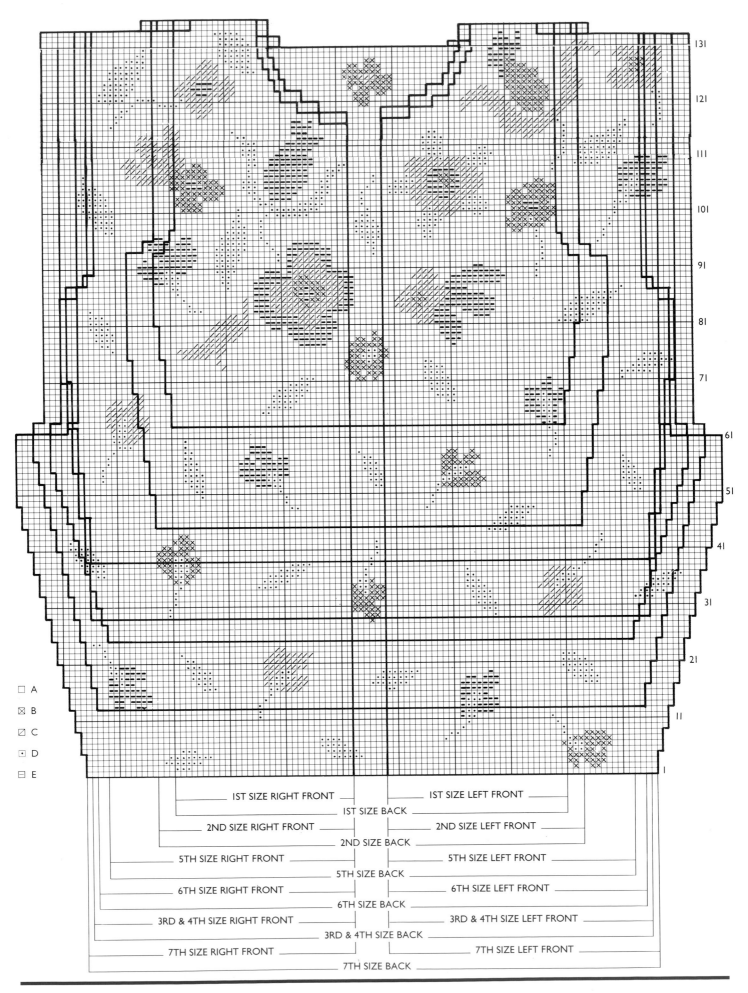

131
121
111
101
91
81
71
61
51
41
31
21
11
1

□ A
⊠ B
⬙ C
⊡ D
⊟ E

1ST SIZE RIGHT FRONT _____ 1ST SIZE LEFT FRONT _____
1ST SIZE BACK _____
2ND SIZE RIGHT FRONT _____ 2ND SIZE LEFT FRONT _____
2ND SIZE BACK _____
5TH SIZE RIGHT FRONT _____ 5TH SIZE LEFT FRONT _____
5TH SIZE BACK _____
6TH SIZE RIGHT FRONT _____ 6TH SIZE LEFT FRONT _____
6TH SIZE BACK _____
3RD & 4TH SIZE RIGHT FRONT _____ 3RD & 4TH SIZE LEFT FRONT _____
3RD & 4TH SIZE BACK _____
7TH SIZE RIGHT FRONT _____ 7TH SIZE LEFT FRONT _____
7TH SIZE BACK _____

74

Design Nº 15

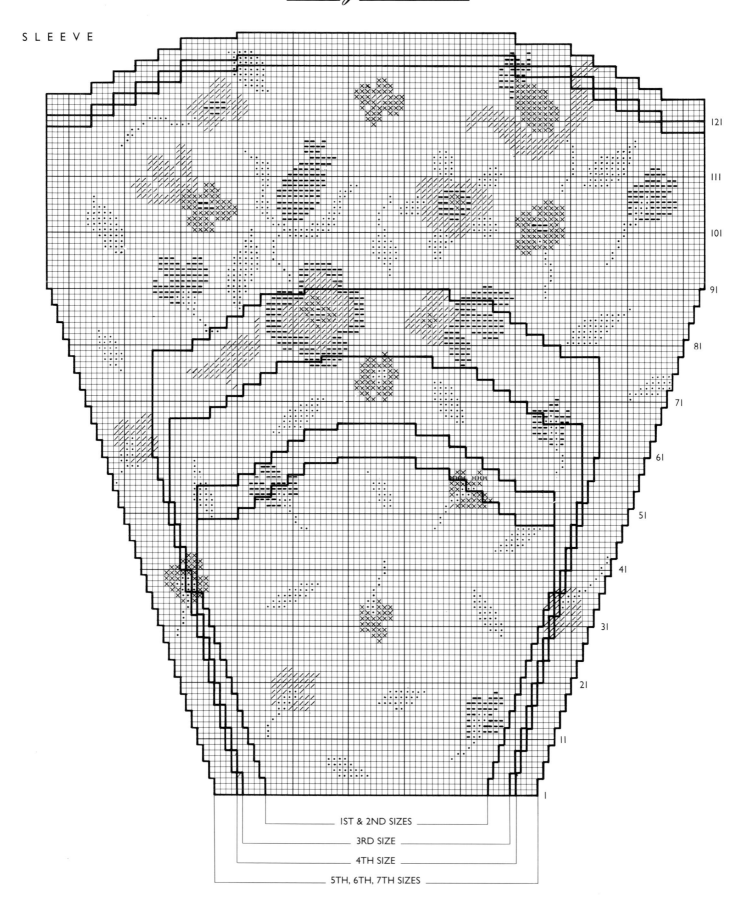

121
111
101
91
81
71
61
51
41
31
21
11
1

1ST & 2ND SIZES

3RD SIZE

4TH SIZE

5TH, 6TH, 7TH SIZES

'When I was a child my parents were based all over Europe. In order to provide stable schooling for my sister and myself, we were sent to a beautiful convent in Belgium. There I had my first invaluable lessons in the needlecrafts.
The religious ceremonies that were a part of convent life, with their elaborate robes and treasures, left an indelible impression on me. I have recreated the sumptuous bejewelled fabrics that I remember so well in these beaded cardigans.'

Shape armholes

Cast off 2[3:3:3:3:3:3] sts at beg of next 2 rows, 1[2:2:2:2:2:2] sts at beg of foll 2 rows and 1[0:0:0:0:0:0] st at beg of next 2 rows. 68[76:98:100:104:110:116] sts. Cont without shaping until Chart row 130 has been completed, so ending with a P row.

Shape shoulders and back neck

Next row Patt 19[21:32:33:35:38:41] sts, turn and complete right side of neck first.
Next row Cast off 2 sts, patt to end.

1st and 2nd sizes only
Work 2 more rows straight (for other side of neck, work one row here). Cast off rem 17[19] sts.

3rd, 4th, 5th, 6th and 7th sizes only
Cast off 15[16:17:18:20] sts at beg of next row. Work one row. Cast off rem 15[15:16:18:19] sts.

All sizes
With RS of work facing, sl centre 30[34:34:34:34:34:34] sts on to a holder, rejoin yarn to next st and patt to end. Work one row, then complete as given for other side of neck, noting the bracketed exception.

LEFT FRONT

Using 3¼mm (US3) needles and A, cast on 32[34:46:46:44:46:48] sts. Work 7cm (2¾in) in rib as given for Back, ending with a WS row and inc one st at end of last row for 2nd, 3rd and 4th sizes only. 32[35:47:47:44:46:48] sts.
Change to 4mm (US6) needles.
Beg with a K row, cont in st st and patt from Chart, starting at row 63[45:39:29:25:13:1]. Work 6[6:8:10:3:4:4] rows. Inc one st at beg (for Right Front, read 'end' here) of next and every foll 6th[6th:8th:8th:3rd:4th:4th] row until there are 35[40:51:52:54:57:60] sts. Cont without shaping until Chart row

The all-over floral pattern of this 'Natasha' cardigan is quite subtle against the deep red background. Outlining the flowers and leaves on the yoke with gold, silver, green, red and white beads, and scattering them over the rest of the fabric at random, makes a glittering glamorous designer creation that will draw admiring glances.

92[92:86:84:60:60:60] (row 93[93:87:85:61:61:61] for Right Front) has been completed, so ending at side edge.

Shape armhole

Cast off 2[3:3:3:3:3:3] sts at beg of next row, 1[2:2:2:2:2:2] sts at beg of foll alt row and 1[0:0:0:0:0:0] st at beg of next alt row. 31[35:46:47:49:52:55] sts. Cont without shaping until Chart row 117 (row 118 for Right Front) has been completed, so ending at front edge.

Shape neck

Cast off at beg of next and foll alt rows 5 sts once, 3[5:4:4:4:4:4] sts once, 3 sts once and one st 3[3:4:4:4:4:4] times. 17[19:30:31:33:36:39] sts.
1st and 2nd sizes only
Work 4 more rows straight (for Right Front, work 3 rows here). Cast off.
3rd, 4th, 5th, 6th and 7th sizes only
Work 2 more rows straight, so ending at armhole edge.

Shape shoulder

Cast off 15[16:17:18:20] sts at beg of next row. Work one row. Cast off rem 15[15:16:18:19] sts.

RIGHT FRONT

Work as given for Left Front, noting the bracketed exceptions.

SLEEVES

Using 3¼mm (US3) needles and A, cast on 36[36:42:44:48:48:48] sts. Work 7cm (2¾in) in rib as given for Back, ending with a RS row.
Next row Rib 4[4:3:4:5:5:5], inc in next st, (rib 8[8:6:6:3:3:3], inc in next st) to last 4[4:3:4:6:6:6] sts, rib to end. 40[40:48:50:58:58:58] sts.
Change to 4mm (US6) needles.
Beg with a K row, cont in st st and patt from Chart, inc one st at each end of

4th[4th:5th:5th:4th:4th:4th] row and every
foll 3rd[3rd:4th:4th:3rd:3rd:3rd] row until
there are 64[64:74:80:118:118:118] sts. Cont
without shaping until Chart row
48[54:66:78:118:120:124] has been
completed, so ending with a P row.

Shape top
Cast off 7[7:7:7:8:8:8] sts at beg of next 2
rows, 3[3:3:3:4:4:4] sts at beg of foll 8 rows
and 6[6:8:8:10:10:10] sts at beg of next 2
rows. Cast off rem 14[14:20:26:50:50:50] sts.

BUTTON BAND

Using 3¼mm (US3) needles and A, cast on 7
sts.
1st row (RS) K1, (P1, K1) to end.
2nd row K1, (K1, P1) to end.
Rep these 2 rows (or work in twisted rib as
set) until band, when slightly stretched, fits
up Left Front edge to start of neck shaping,
ending with a WS row. Cut off yarn. Leave sts
on a safety-pin.
Sew band in position. Mark position of
5[6:6:7:7:8:8] buttons with pins – the first to
come 1cm (½in) above lower edge and the
last 4[5:5:5:5:5:5]cm (1½[2:2:2:2:2:2]in) from
top of band, with the others evenly spaced
between.

BUTTONHOLE BAND

Work as given for Button Band until band fits
up Right Front edge to start of neck shaping,
ending with RS row. Do not cut off yarn.
Make buttonholes as markers are reached as
foll:
Buttonhole row (RS) Rib 3, yo, work 2 tog,
rib to end.
Sew band in position.

NECKBAND

Join shoulder seams.
Using 3¼mm (US3) needle holding
buttonhole band sts and with RS of work
facing, pick up and K20[23:23:23:23:23:23]
sts up right front neck, 3 sts down right back

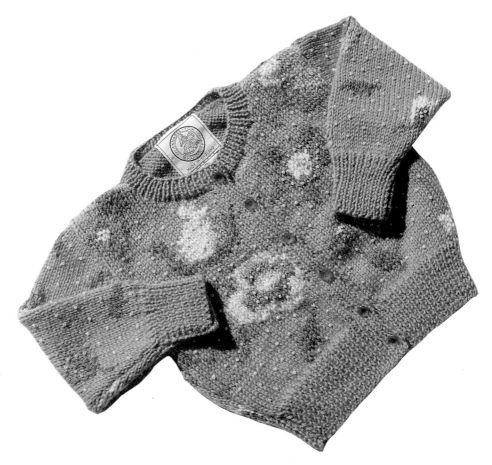

neck, K across back neck sts on holder inc
one st at centre, pick up and K3 sts up left
back neck, 20[23:23:23:23:23:23] sts down
left front neck and rib across 7 button band
sts from safety-pin.
91[101:101:101:101:101:101] sts.
Work 2cm (¾in) in rib as set, making
buttonhole as before on second row. Cast off
evenly in rib.

TO MAKE UP

Press on WS of work using a warm iron over
a damp cloth. If required, sew beads at
random over Back, Fronts and Sleeves of
child's cardigan or use beads to outline and
detail flower and leaf shapes on Back and
Fronts of ladies' cardigan and sew some
randomly and in clusters as shown to form a
yoke effect. Set in sleeves. Join side and sleeve
seams. Press seams. Sew on buttons.

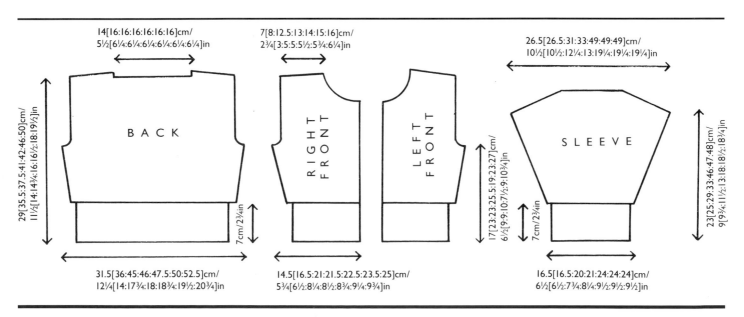

Design N.º 16

Hudson

This is a sweater that is reminiscent of traditional British knitwear with interesting stitches and texture rather than colour and patterns. Rowan Designer DK shows the cable panels and moss stitch diamonds to perfection, while the zig-zag pattern and rib cuffs plus neckband add a stylish dimension to a classic garment.

SIZES

To fit chest 97[102:107]cm (38[40:42]in)
Actual size 103[107:114]cm (40½[42:45]in)
Length to shoulder 67[67:71]cm (26½[26½:28]in)
Sleeve seam 52[52:54]cm (20½[20½:21¼]in)
Figures in square brackets [] refer to larger sizes; where there is only one set of figures, it applies to all sizes

MATERIALS

16[17:18] × 50g balls of Rowan Designer DK
Pair each of 3¼mm (US3) and 4mm (US6) knitting needles and a cable needle

TENSION

28 sts and 32 rows to 10cm (4in) over patt using 4mm (US6) needles

SPECIAL ABBREVIATIONS

RT = right twist: K next 2 sts tog leaving sts on left-hand needle; insert right-hand needle from the front between two sts just knitted tog and K the first st again, then slip both sts off needle tog.
LT = left twist: with right-hand needle behind left-hand needle, miss next st and K second st tbl; then insert right-hand needle into backs of both sts (the missed st and second st) and K2 tog tbl.

BACK

Using 3¼mm (US3) needles cast on 112[120:120] sts. P 4 rows. Cont in K1, P1 rib until work measures 5cm (2in) from beg, ending with a WS row. P 4 more rows. Change to 4mm (US6) needles.

Commence zig-zag patt.
1st row (RS) (K2, RT, LT, K2) to end.
2nd row P to end.
3rd row (K1, RT, K2, LT, K1) to end.
4th row P to end.
5th row (RT, K4, LT) to end.
6th row K to end.
K one row.
Next row K9[2:1], inc in next st, (K2[3:2], inc in next st) to last 9[1:1] sts, K9[[1:1]. 144[150:160] sts.
Cont in patt from Chart, reading odd-numbered (RS) rows from right to left and even-numbered (WS) rows from left to right. Set patt as foll:
1st row (RS) Moss st 1[4:9] sts, work 1st row of Chart to last 2[5:10] sts, moss st 2[5:10].
Cont in patt until work measures 42[42:46]cm (16½[16½:18]in) from beg, ending with a WS row.

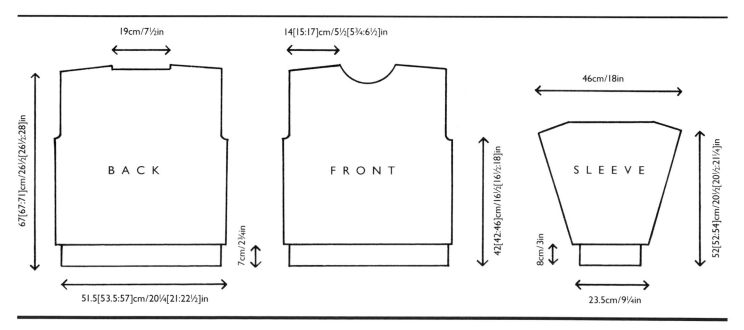

BACK — 67[67:71]cm/26½[26½:28]in · 51.5[53.5:57]cm/20¼[21:22½]in · 7cm/2¾in · 19cm/7½in

FRONT — 14[15:17]cm/5½[5¾:6½]in · 42[42:46]cm/16½[16½:18]in

SLEEVE — 46cm/18in · 52[52:54]cm/20½[20½:21¼]in · 8cm/3in · 23.5cm/9¼in

Design Nº 16

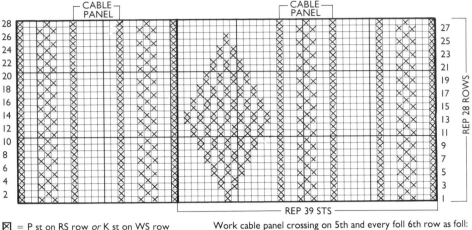

⊠ = P st on RS row *or* K st on WS row

☐ = K st on RS row *or* P st on WS row

Work cable panel crossing on 5th and every foll 6th row as foll:
sl next 3 sts onto cable needle and leave at front of work, K3,
then K3 from cable needle.

Shape armholes
Keeping patt correct, cast off 3 sts at beg of
next 4 rows. 132[138:148] sts. *
Cont without shaping until work measures
67[67:71]cm (26½[26½:28]in) from beg,
ending with a WS row.

Shape shoulders and back neck
Next row Cast off 20[21:24] sts, patt until
there are 19[21:23] sts on right-hand needle,
turn.
Work one row. Cast off rem 19[21:23] sts.
With RS of work facing, sl centre 54 sts on to
a holder, rejoin yarn to next st and patt to
end.
Next row Cast off 20[21:24] sts, patt to end.
Work one row. Cast off rem 19[21:23] sts.

FRONT

Work as given for Back to *.
Cont without shaping until armholes measure
19cm (7½in) from beg, ending with a WS
row.

Shape neck
Next row Patt 57[60:65] sts, turn and leave
rem sts on a spare needle.
Complete left side of neck first.
Cast off at beg of next and foll alt rows 4 sts 3
times, 2 sts twice and one st twice.
39[42:47] sts.
Cont without shaping until Front matches
Back to shoulder, ending at armhole edge.

Shape shoulder
Cast off 20[21:24] sts at beg of next row.
Work one row. Cast off rem 19[21:23] sts.
With RS of work facing, sl centre 18 sts on to
a holder, rejoin yarn to next st and patt to
end. Work one row, then complete as given
for other side of neck.

SLEEVES

Using 3¼mm (US3) needles cast on 48 sts. P
4 rows. Work 1st-5th rows as given for zig-
zag patt on Back. P 5 more rows. Work 6
rows in K1, P1 rib. P 4 rows.
Change to 4mm (US6) needles.
Work 6 rows zig-zag patt as given for Back. K
one row.
Next row K6, inc in next st, (K1, inc in next
st) to last 7 sts, K7. 66 sts.
Cont from Chart, setting patt as foll:
1st row (RS) K2, work 1st row of Chart to last
st, K1.
Cont in patt, inc one st at each end of 5th and
every foll 4th row until there are 128 sts,
working extra sts into diamond patt and moss
st.
Cont without shaping until sleeve measures
52[52:54]cm (20½[20½:21¼]in) from beg,
ending with a WS row.

Shape top
Cast off 6 sts at beg of next 4 rows, 4 sts at
beg of foll 6 rows and 12 sts at beg of next 2
rows. Cast off rem 56 sts.

NECKBAND

Join right shoulder seam.
Using 3¼mm (US3) needles and with RS of
work facing, pick up and K27 sts down left
front neck, K across 18 sts on holder, pick up
and K27 sts up right front neck, one st down
right back neck, K across 54 sts on holder
and pick up and K one st up left back neck.
128 sts.
K 3 rows. Work 1st-5th rows as given for zig-
zag patt on Back. P 5 rows. Work 6 rows zig-
zag patt as given for Back. P 4 more rows.
Work 5cm (2in) in K1, P1 rib. Cast off loosely
in rib.

TO MAKE UP

Press lightly on WS using a warm iron over a
dry cloth. Join left shoulder and neckband
seam. Fold neckband in half to inside and slip
stitch in position. Set in sleeves. Join side and
sleeve seams. Press seams.

Design Nº 17

Sweetheart

An irresistible design in a lightweight double knitting to suit a mother and her daughter. The adult's sweater with its array of cable and stitchwork panels has a crew neck, while the child's version has a moss stitch collar.

SIZES

Child's sweater
To fit chest 51[56:61-66-66:71]cm (20[22:24-26:26-28]in)
Actual size 57[64:74:91]cm (22½[25:29:32]in)
Length to shoulder 36[39:44:49]cm (14[15¼:17¼:19¼]in)
Sleeve seam 20[25.5:30:35]cm (7¾[10:11¾:13¾]in)

Ladies' sweater
To fit bust 87-91[91-97:97-102]cm (34-36[36-38:38-40]in)
Actual size 108[112:117]cm (42½[44:46]in)
Length to shoulder 60[62:65]cm (23½[24½:25½]in)
Sleeve seam 47[48:49]cm (18½[18¾:19¼]in)
Figures in square brackets [] refer to larger sizes; where there is only one set of figures, it applies to all sizes

MATERIALS

Child's sweater
10[12:14:16] × 25g hanks of Rowan Lightweight DK in shade 20
Pair each of 3¼mm (US3) and 3¾mm (US5) knitting needles
3¼mm (US3) circular knitting needle
Cable needle

Ladies' sweater
14[15:16] × 50g balls of Rowan Designer DK in shade 615
Pair each of 3¼mm (US3) and 4mm (US6) knitting needles
Cable needle

TENSION

Child's sweater
29½ sts and 36 rows to 10cm (4in) over patt using 3¾mm (US5) needles

Ladies' sweater
26 sts and 32 rows to 10cm (4in) over patt using 4mm (US6) needles

Combining cable and stitchwork panels is an interesting exercise resulting in these pretty sweaters worn by Tijan and Frances. Frances' sweater has five panels across the front and back with the evocatively named 'Nosegay Pattern' with its sprigs of textured flowers at the centre front.

SPECIAL ABBREVIATIONS

RT = right twist: K2 tog leaving sts on left-hand needle, insert right-hand needle from front between sts just knitted tog and K the first st again, then sl both sts from needle tog
LT = left twist: with the right-hand needle behind the left-hand needle, miss one st and K the second st tbl, then insert the right-hand needle into backs of both sts and K2 tog tbl
FC = front cross: sl next st on to cable needle and leave at front of work, P1, then K1 from cable needle
FKC = front knit cross: work as FC, but *knit* both sts
BC = back cross: sl next st on to cable needle and leave at back of work, K1, then P1 from cable needle
BKC = back knit cross: work as BC, but *knit* both sts
MB = make bobble: (K1, P1) twice into same st, turn and P4, turn and K4, turn and (P2 tog) twice, turn and K2 tog
cd inc = central double increase: (K1 tbl, K1) into next st, then insert the left-hand needle point behind the vertical strand that runs downward from between the 2 sts just made, then K1 tbl into this strand to make the 3rd st of the group
ssk = slip, slip, knit: sl the first and second st one at a time as if to knit, then insert point of left-hand needle into fronts of these 2 sts and K them tog
2BC = slip next st on to cable needle and leave at back of work, K2, then P1 from cable needle
2FC = sl next 2 sts on to cable needle and leave at front of work, P1, then K2 from cable needle
C4B = sl next 2 sts on to cable needle and leave at back of work, K2, then K 2 sts from cable needle
C4F = sl next 2 sts on to cable needle and leave at front of work, K2, then K 2 sts from cable needle

HEART PANEL

(Worked over 14 sts – called patt 14 in the instructions)
1st and every foll alt row (WS) K2, P10, K2.
2nd row P2, K3, RT, LT, K3, P2.
4th row P2, K2, RT, K2, LT, K2, P2.
6th row P2, K1, RT, K4, LT, K1, P2.
8th row P2, RT, K6, LT, P2.
10th row As 2nd.
12th row P2, LT, RT, K2, LT, RT, P2.
14th row P2, K1, M1, K2 tog tbl, K4, K2 tog, M1, K1, P2.

16th row P2, K10, P2.
Rep these 16 rows to form patt.

NOSEGAY PATTERN

(Worked over 16 sts – called patt 16 in the instructions)
1st row (WS) K7, P2, K7.
2nd row P6, BKC, FKC, P6.
3rd row K5, FC, P2, BC, K5.
4th row P4, BC, BKC, FKC, FC, P4.
5th row K3, FC, K1, P4, K1, BC, K3.
6th row P2, BC, P1, BC, K2, FC, P1, FC, P2.
7th row (K2, P1) twice, K1, P2, K1, (P1, K2) twice
8th row P2, MB, P1, BC, P1, K2, P1, FC, P1, MB, P2.
9th row K4, P1, K2, P2, K2, P1, K4.
10th row P4, MB, P2, K2, P2, MB, P4.
Rep these 10 rows to form patt.

EMBOSSED HEART

(Worked over 15 sts, inc to 21 – called patt 15 in the instructions)
1st row (WS) K15.
2nd row P15.
3rd row K15.
4th row P7, cd inc, P7.
5th row K7, P3, K7.
6th row P5, P2 tog, K1, cd inc, K1, P2 tog, P5.
7th row K6, P5, K6.
8th row P4, P2 tog, K2, cd inc, K2, P2 tog, P4.
9th row K5, P7, K5.
10th row P3, P2 tog, K3, cd inc, K3, P2 tog, P3.
11th row K4, P9, K4.
12th row P4, K4, cd inc, K4, P4.
13th row K4, P5, K1, P5, K4.
14th row P4, K5, (P1, yo, P1) into next st, K5, P4.
15th row K4, P5, K3, P5, K4.
16th row P4, ssk, K3 tog, pass the ssk st over the K3 tog st, inc 1 (by purling into front and back of st), P1, inc 1, ssk, K3 tog, pass the ssk st over the K3 tog st, P4.
Rep these 16 rows to form patt.

DOUBLE CABLE

(Worked over 12 sts – called patt 12 in the instructions)
1st row (WS) K2, P8, K2.
2nd row P2, C4B, C4F, P2.
3rd row K2, P8, K2.
4th row P2, K8, P2.
5th–8th rows Rep 3rd and 4th rows twice.
Rep these 8 rows to form patt.

VALENTINE CABLE

(Worked over 16 sts – called patt 16VC in the instructions)
1st row (WS) K6, P4, K6.
2nd row P6, C4F, P6.
3rd row As 1st.
4th row P5, 2BC, 2FC, P5.
5th row K5, P2, K2, P2, K5.
6th row P4, 2BC, P2, 2FC, P4.
7th row (K4, P2) twice, K4.
8th row P3, 2BC, P4, 2FC, P3.
9th row K3, P2, K6, P2, K3.
10th row P2, (2BC) twice, (2FC) twice, P2.
11th row K2, (P2, K1, P2, K2) twice.
12th row P1, (2BC) twice, P2, (2FC) twice, P1.
13th row (K1, P2) twice, K4, (P2, K1) twice.
14th row P1, K1, FC, 2FC, P2, 2BC, BC, K1, P1.
15th row (K1, P1) twice, K1, P2, K2, P2, K1, (P1, K1) twice.
16th row P1, K1, P1, FC, 2FC, 2BC, BC, P1, K1, P1.
17th row K1, P1, K2, P1, K1, P4, K1, P1, K2, P1, K1.
18th row P1, FC, BC, P1, C4F, P1, FC, BC, P1.
19th row K2, BKC, K2, P4, K2, FKC, K2.
Rep 4th–19th rows to form patt.

The larger-size adult's version of the 'Sweetheart' sweater has space for nine panels across the front and back in a different arrangement to the child's sweater.

CHILD'S SWEATER

BACK

Using 3¼mm (US3) needles cast on 76[82:98:104] sts. Work 4[4:5:6]cm (1½[1½:2:2½]in) in K1, P1 rib, ending with a WS row.
Next row K6[7:5:7], inc in next st, (K8[5:7:5], inc in next st) to last 6[8:4:6] sts, K to end. 84[94:110:120] sts.
Change to 3¾mm (US5) needles.
Commence patt.
1st row (WS) K4[9:7:10], P0[0:3:3], K0[0:7:9], P1, work 1st row patt 12, P1, work 1st row patt 15, P1, work 1st row patt 16, P1, work 1st row patt 15, P1, work 1st row patt 12, P1, K0[0:7:9], P0[0:3:3], K4[9:7:10].
2nd row P4[9:7:10], K0[0:1:1], P0[0:1:1], K0[0:1:1], P0[0:7:9], K1, work 2nd row patt 12, K1, work 2nd row patt 15, K1, work 2nd row patt 16, K1, work 2nd row patt 15, K1, work 2nd row patt 12, K1, P0[0:7:9], K0[0:1:1], P0[0:1:1], K0[0:1:1], P4[9:7:10].
These 2 rows set patt. Cont in patt until work measures 23[24:28:32]cm (9[9½:11:12½]in) from beg, ending with a WS row.

Shape armholes
Cast off 2[2:3:3] sts at beg of next 2 rows and 1[2:2:2] sts at beg of foll 2 rows.
78[86:100:110] sts.
Cont with shaping until work measures 36[39:44:49]cm (14[15¼:17¼:19¼]in) from beg, ending with a WS row.

Shape shoulders and back neck
Next row Cast off 11[12:15:17] sts, patt until there are 10[11:14:17] sts on right-hand needle, turn.
Work one row.
Cast off rem 10[11:14:17] sts.
With RS of work facing, sl centre 36[40:42:42] sts on to a holder, rejoin yarn to next st and patt to end.
Next row Cast off 11[12:15:17] sts, patt to end.
Work one row. Cast off rem 10[11:14:17] sts.

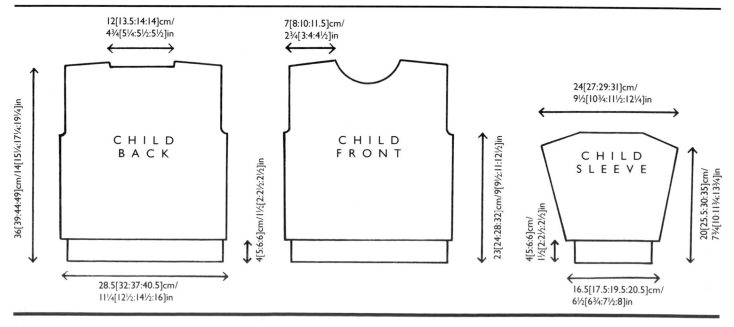

12[13.5:14:14]cm/
4¾[5¼:5½:5½]in

7[8:10:11.5]cm/
2¾[3:4:4½]in

36[39:44:49]cm/14[15¼:17¼:19¼]in

CHILD BACK

28.5[32:37:40.5]cm/
11¼[12½:14½:16]in

4[5:6:6]cm/1½[2:2½:2½]in

CHILD FRONT

23[24:28:32]cm/9[9½:11:12½]in

4[5:6:6]cm/1½[2:2½:2½]in

24[27:29:31]cm/
9½[10¾:11½:12¼]in

CHILD SLEEVE

20[25.5:30:35]cm/
7¾[10:11¾:13¾]in

16.5[17.5:19.5:20.5]cm/
6½[6¾:7½:8]in

Design N° 17

FRONT

Work as given for Back until work measures 32[35:39:44]cm (12½[13¾:15¼:17¼]in) from beg, ending with a WS row.

Shape neck

Next row Patt 33[36:43:48] sts, turn and leave rem sts on a spare needle.
Complete left side of neck first. Cast off at beg of next and foll alt rows 5[6:5:5] sts once, 3 sts once, 2 sts once, 1[1:2:2] sts once, one st once and 0[0:1:1] st once. 21[23:29:34] sts.
Cont without shaping until Front matches Back to shoulder, ending at armhole edge.

Shape shoulder

Cast off 11[12:15:17] sts at beg of next row.
Work one row. Cast off rem 10[11:14:17] sts.
With RS of work facing, sl centre 12[14:14:14] sts on to a holder, rejoin yarn to next st and patt to end. Work one row, then complete as given for other side of neck.

SLEEVES

Using 3¼mm (US3) needles cast on 38[40:44:46] sts. Work 4[4:5:6]cm (1½[1½:2:2½]in) in K1, P1 rib, ending with a WS row.
Next row K5[5:4:5], inc in next st, (K8[9:6:6], inc in next st) to last 5[4:4:5] sts, K to end. 42[44:50:52] sts.
Change to 3¾mm (US5) needles.
Commence patt.

1st size only
1st row (WS) Work last 12 sts of 1st row patt 15, P1, work 1st row patt 16, P1, work first 12 sts of 1st row patt 15.

2nd size only
1st row (WS) Work last 13 sts of 1st row patt 15, P1, work 1st row patt 16, P1, work first 13 sts of 1st row patt 15.

3rd size only
1st row (WS) P1, work 1st row patt 15, P1, work 1st row patt 16, P1, work 1st row patt 15, P1.

4th size only
1st row (WS) K1, P1, work 1st row patt 15, P1, work 1st row patt 16, P1, work 1st row patt 15, P1, K1.

All sizes
This row sets patt.
Cont in patt, inc one st at each end of 4th[4th:5th:5th] and every foll 3rd[3rd:4th:4th] row until there are 70[80:86:92] sts.
Work extra sts into patt as foll: **1st and 2nd sizes only** Complete patt 15 and work K1 (RS) line on either side as for Back, then work rem sts in reverse st st. **3rd and 4th sizes only** Introduce patt 12 on either side as you inc and work K1 (RS) line on either side as for Back, then work rem sts in reverse st st.
Cont in patt without shaping until work measures 20[25.5:30:35]cm (7¾[10:11¾:13¾]in) from beg, ending with a WS row.

Shape top
Cast off 5[6:6:6] sts at beg of next 2 rows, 4 sts at beg of foll 6[6:10:10] rows and 7[8:7:8] sts at beg of next 2 rows. Cast off rem 22[28:20:24] sts.

COLLAR

Join shoulder seams.
Using 3¼mm (US3) circular needle and with RS of work facing, beg at left shoulder and pick up and K18[20:22:22] sts down left front neck, K across 12[14:14:14] sts on holder, pick up and K18[20:22:22] sts up right front neck, 2 sts down right back neck, K across 36[40:42:42] sts on holder and pick up and K 2 sts up left back neck. 90[100:104:104] sts.
Work 3cm (1¼in) in rounds of moss st, ending at left shoulder.
Divide for collar
Next row Patt 24[27:29:29] sts, turn.
Work a further 5[5:6:6]cm (2[2:2½:2½]in) backwards and forwards in rows of moss st. Cast off.

TO MAKE UP

Press very lightly on WS of work. Set in sleeves. Join side and sleeve seams. Press seams.

LADIES' SWEATER

BACK

Using 3¼mm (US3) needles cast on 112[118:122] sts.
1st row (RS) (K1 tbl, P1) to end.
Rep this row to form twisted rib for 7cm (2¾in), ending with a WS row.
Next row K2[4:2], inc in next st, (K3, inc in next st) to last 1[5:3] sts, K to end. 140[146:152] sts.
Change to 4mm (US6) needles.
Commence patt.
1st row (WS) K1[4:7], P1, work 1st row patt 14, P1, work 1st row patt 16, P1, work 1st row patt 15, P1, work 1st row patt 12, work 1st row patt 16VC, work 1st row patt 12, P1, work 1st row patt 15, P1, work 1st row patt 16, P1, work 1st row patt 14, P1, K1[4:7].
2nd row P1[4:7], K1, work 2nd row patt 14, K1, work 2nd row patt 16, K1, work 2nd row patt 15, K1, work 2nd row patt 12, work 2nd row patt 16VC, work 2nd row patt 12, K1, work 2nd row patt 15, K1, work 2nd row patt 16, K1, work 2nd row patt 14, K1, P1[4:7].
These 2 rows set patt. Cont in patt until work measures 37[39:42]cm (14½[15¼:16½]in) from beg, ending with a WS row.

Shape armholes
Cast off 3 sts at beg of next 2 rows and 2 sts at beg of foll 2 rows. 130[136:142] sts. Cont without shaping until work measures 60[62:65]cm (23½[24½:25½]in) from beg, ending with a WS row.

Shape shoulders and back neck
Next row Cast off 21[23:24] sts, patt until there are 21[22:24] sts on right-hand needle, turn.
Work one row. Cast off rem 21[22:24] sts.
With RS of work facing, sl centre 46 sts on to a holder, rejoin yarn to next st and patt to end.
Next row Cast off 21[23:24] sts, patt to end.
Work one row. Cast off rem 21[22:24] sts.

FRONT

Work as given for Back until work measures 55[57:59]cm (21½[22½:23¼]in) from beg, ending with a WS row.

Shape neck
Next row Patt 60[63:66] sts, turn and leave rem sts on a spare needle.

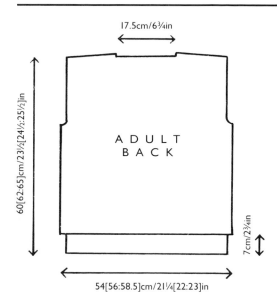

17.5cm/6¾in

16[17.5:18.5]cm/6¼[6¾:7¼]in

47cm/18½in

ADULT
BACK

ADULT
FRONT

ADULT
SLEEVE

60[62:65]cm/23½[24½:25½]in

37[39:42]cm/14½[15¼:16½]in

47[48:49]cm/18½[18¾:19¼]in

7cm/2¾in

7cm/2¾in

54[56:58.5]cm/21¼[22:23]in

24cm/9½in

Cast off at beg of next and foll alt rows 6 sts once, 4 sts once, 3 sts once, 2 sts twice and one st once. 42[45:48] sts. Cont without shaping until work matches Back to shoulder, ending at armhole edge.

Shape shoulder

Cast off 21[23:24] sts at beg of next row. Work one row. Cast off rem 21[22:24] sts. With RS of work facing, sl centre 10 sts on to a holder, rejoin yarn to next st and patt to end. Work one row, then complete as given for other side of neck.

SLEEVES

Using 3¼mm (US3) needles cast on 50 sts. Work 7cm (2¾in) in twisted rib as given for Back, ending with a WS row.
Next row (K3, inc in next st) to last 2 sts, K2. 62 sts.
Change to 4mm (US6) needles.
Commence patt.
1st row (WS) Work last 10 sts of 1st row patt 15, P1, work 1st row patt 12, work 1st row patt 16VC, work 1st row patt 12, P1, work first 10 sts of 1st row patt 15.
This row sets patt. Cont in patt, inc one st at each end of every 3rd row until there are 122 sts. Work extra sts into patt as foll: complete the rest of patt 15 as you inc, working K1 (RS) line on either side of patt, then work rem inc sts in reverse st st. Cont in patt until work measures 47[48:49]cm (18½[18¾:19¼]in) from beg, ending with a WS row.

Shape top

Cast off 8 sts at beg of next 2 rows, 4 sts at beg of foll 6 rows, 6 sts at beg of next 2 rows and 10 sts at beg of foll 2 rows. Cast off rem 50 sts.

NECKBAND

Join right shoulder seam.
Using 3¼mm (US3) needles and with RS of work facing, pick up and K30 sts down left front neck, K across 10 sts from holder, pick up and K30 sts up right front neck, 2 sts down right back neck, K across 46 sts from

'The versatility of using knitted stitchwork in a solid colour to form a beautiful pattern never ceases to amaze me. The contrast of embossed textures and shadows makes a very rich fabric that is completely different to my other designs that involve masses of colour and motifs. 'Sweetheart' is a combination of some of my favourite stitches that have such evocative names as 'Nosegay Pearl' and 'Embossed Heart'.'

holder and pick up and K 2 sts up left back neck. 120 sts.
Work 6cm (2½in) in twisted rib. Cast off loosely in rib.

TO MAKE UP

Press lightly on WS of work. Join left shoulder and neckband seam. Fold neckband in half to inside and slip stitch in position. Set in sleeves. Join side and sleeve seams. Press seams.

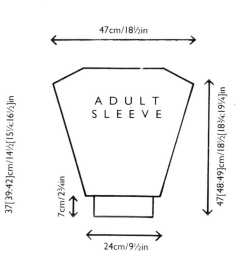

White VINE

A stitchwork pattern of trailing leaves and cable panels gives this sweater and cardigan a sculptured surface. Using Rowan's popular pure wool Designer DK for maximum effect, the design also incorporates an unusual deep ruffled hem and neat moss stitch collar.

SIZES

To fit bust 81-87[87-91:96-102]cm (32-34[34-36:38-40]in)
Actual size 131[131:135]cm (51½[51½:53]in)
Length to shoulder 63[65:69]cm (24¾[25½:27]in)
Sleeve seam 39.5[39.5:40.5]cm (15½[15½:16]in)
Figures in square brackets [] refer to larger sizes; where there is only one set of figures, it applies to all sizes

MATERIALS

17[17:18] × 50g balls of Designer DK
Pair each of 3¼mm (US3) and 4mm (US6) knitting needles
4mm (US6) circular knitting needle (long)
3¼mm (US3) circular knitting needle for collar of sweater
Cable needle
6 buttons for cardigan

TENSION

25 sts and 31 rows to 10cm (4in) over patt using 4mm (US6) needles

NOTE

Commence work using circular needle (working to and fro in rows) to cope with large number of sts. Change to pair of needles when sts reduce after ruffled welt.

CABLE PANEL

(Worked over 12 sts)
1st row (WS) P2, K1, P6, K1, P2.
2nd row K2, P1, K6, P1, K2.
3rd and 4th rows As 1st and 2nd.
5th row As 1st.
6th row K2, P1, sl next 3 sts on to cable needle and leave at front of work, K3, then K 3 sts from cable needle, P1, K2.
Rep these 6 rows to form patt.

TRAILING LEAVES PANEL

(Worked over 26 sts – Note that sts are increased and decreased within panel. St checks in the pattern do not take any increased sts into account)
1st row (WS) K5, P5, K4, P3, K9.
2nd row P7, P2 tog, K into front and back of next st, K2, P4, K2, yo, K1, yo, K2, P5.
3rd row K5, P7, K4, P2, K1, P1, K8.
4th row P6, P2 tog, K1, P into front and back of next st – called P inc, K2, P4, K3, yo, K1, yo, K3, P5.
5th row K5, P9, K4, P2, K2, P1, K7.
6th row P5, P2 tog, K1, P inc, P1, K2, P4, sl next 2 sts K-wise on to right-hand needle, then K these tog through first st – called SSK, K5, K2 tog, P5.
7th row K5, P7, K4, P2, K3, P1, K6.
8th row P4, P2 tog, K1, P inc, P2, K2, P4, SSK, K3, K2 tog, P5.
9th row K5, P5, K4, P2, K4, P1, K5.
10th row P5, yo, K1, yo, P4, K2, P4, SSK, K1, K2 tog, P5.
11th row K5, P3, K4, P2, K4, P3, K5.
12th row P5, (K1, yo) twice, K1, P4, K1, pick up loop lying between needles and K tbl – called make 1 (M1), K1, P2 tog, P2, sl 2 K-wise, K1, pass slipped sts over – called p2sso, P5.
13th row K9, P3, K4, P5, K5.
14th row P5, K2, yo, K1, yo, K2, P4, K1, K into front and back of next st, K1, P2 tog, P7.
15th row K8, P1, K1, P2, K4, P7, K5.
16th row P5, K3, yo, K1, yo, K3, P4, K2, P inc, K1, P2 tog, P6.
17th row K7, P1, K2, P2, K4, P9, K5.
18th row P5, SSK, K5, K2 tog, P4, K2, P1, P inc, K1, P2 tog, P5.
19th row K6, P1, K3, P2, K4, P7, K5.
20th row P5, SSK, K3, K2 tog, P4, K2, P2, P inc, K1, P2 tog, P4.
21st row K5, P1, K4, P2, K4, P5, K5.
22nd row P5, SSK, K1, K2 tog, P4, K2, P4, yo, K1, yo, P5.
23rd row K5, P3, K4, P2, K4, P3, K5.
24th row P5, sl 2 K-wise, K1, p2sso, P2, P2 tog, K1, M1, K1, P4, (K1, yo) twice, K1, P5.
Rep these 24 rows to form patt.

SWEATER

BACK

Using 4mm (US6) circular needle cast on 356[356:367] sts. Commence long ruffle welt patt.
1st row K4, (P7, K4) to end.
2nd row P4, (K7, P4) to end.
3rd-12th rows Rep 1st and 2nd rows 5 times.
13th row As 1st.
14th row P4, (K2, sl 2 K-wise, K1, pass slipped sts over – called p2sso, K2, P4) to end.
15th row K4, (P5, K4) to end.
16th row P4, (K5, P4) to end.
17th-24th rows Rep 15th and 16th rows 4 times.
25th row As 15th.
26th row P4, (K1, sl 2 K-wise, K1, p2sso, K1, P4) to end.
27th row K4, (P3, K4) to end.
28th row P4, (K3, P4) to end.
29th-30th rows As 27th and 28th.
31st row As 27th.
32nd row P4, (sl 2 K-wise, K1, p2sso, P4) to end. 164[164:169] sts.
33rd row K4, (P1 tbl, K4) to end.
34th row P4, (K1, P4) to end.
35th row P to end.
36th row P1, (yo, P2 tog) to last 1[1:0] st, P1[1:0].
37th row P to end. (For Cardigan, P one more row here.)
Commence main body patt.
First two sizes only
1st row (WS) Patt 12 sts as given for 1st row

Pam (left) wears the cardigan with its practical pockets; Monica (right) is in the sweater version of the design.

Design N.º 18

Shape top
Keeping patt correct, cast off 4 sts at beg of next 14 rows and 9 sts at beg of foll 2 rows. Cast off rem 54 sts.

NECKBAND

Join right shoulder seam.
Using 3¼mm (US3) needles and with RS of work facing, * pick up and K 20 sts down left front neck, K across 20[20:21] sts on holder, pick up and K20 sts up right front neck and K across 46[46:47] back neck sts on holder. 106[106:108] sts. *
Work 6cm (2½in) in K1, P1 rib. Cast off in rib.

COLLAR

Join both shoulder seams.
Using 3¼mm (US3) circular needle and with RS of work facing, beg at left shoulder and work as given for neckband from * to *.
Work 3cm (1¼in) in rounds of moss st.

Divide for collar
Next row Moss st 30 sts (to centre front neck), turn.
Cont in rows of moss st until collar measures 10cm (4in) from beg. Cast off in patt.

TO MAKE UP

Join left shoulder and neckband seam on crew neck sweater. Fold neckband in half to inside and slip stitch in position. Set in sleeves. Join side and sleeve seams.

CARDIGAN

BACK

Work as given for Back of Sweater, noting the bracketed exception.

POCKET LININGS
(make 2)

Using 4mm (US6) needles cast on 30 sts. Beg with a K row, work 44 rows in st st. Cut off yarn. Leave sts on a spare needle.

LEFT FRONT

Using 4mm (US6) circular needle cast on 191 sts. Work 37 rows as given for Back ruffle welt patt. 89 sts.
Next row P to end, dec 5[5:3] sts evenly across row. 84[84:86] sts.
Commence main body patt.
1st row (WS) Work 6 sts in moss st and sl these sts on to a safety-pin for Button Band, P2, (patt 26 sts as 1st row of trailing leaves panel, 12 sts as 1st row of cable panel) twice, then for the last size only work 2 sts in moss st. 78[78:80] sts.
Cont in patt as set until work measures 26cm (10¼in) from beg, ending with a WS row.

Place pocket lining
Next row Patt 28 sts, sl next 30 sts on to a holder, K across 30 sts from pocket lining, patt 20[20:22] sts.
Cont without shaping until work matches Back to underarm, ending at side edge.

of cable panel, (patt 26 sts as given for 1st row of trailing leaves panel, 12 sts as given for 1st row of cable panel) 4 times.
Last size only
1st row (WS) Work 3 sts in moss st, then work as given for 1st row of other sizes to last 2 sts, work 2 sts in moss st.
All sizes
2nd row Follow 2nd row of cable and trailing leaves panels in order set out in previous row.
Cont in patt as set until work measures 38[40:44]cm (15[15¾:17¼]in) from beg, ending with a WS row.

Shape armholes
Keeping patt correct, cast off 3 sts at beg of next 4 rows. 152[152:157] sts. *
Cont without shaping until work measures 63[65:69]cm (24¾[25½:27]in) from beg, ending with a WS row.

Shape shoulders
Cast off 26[26:27] sts at beg of next 2 rows and 27[27:28] sts at beg of foll 2 rows. Cut off yarn. Leave rem 46[46:47] sts on a holder.

FRONT

Work as given for Back to *.
Cont without shaping until armholes measure 21cm (8¼in) from beg, ending with a WS row.

Shape neck
Next row Patt 66[66:68] sts, turn and leave rem sts on a spare needle.
Complete left side of neck first.
** Cast off at beg of next and foll alt rows 5

sts once, 4 sts once, 2 sts once and one st twice. 53[53:55] sts. Cont without shaping until Front matches Back to shoulder, ending at armhole edge.

Shape shoulder
Cast off 26[26:27] sts at beg of next row. Work one row. Cast off rem 27[27:28] sts.
With RS of work facing, sl centre 20[20:21] sts on to a holder, rejoin yarn to next st and patt to end. Work one row, then complete as given for other side of neck from ** to end.

SLEEVES

Using 4mm (US6) needles cast on 130 sts. Work 19th-36th rows as given for 1st size Back ruffle welt patt. 74 sts.
Next row P to end, dec 4 sts evenly across row. 70 sts. (For Cardigan P one more row here.)
Commence main patt.
1st row (WS) Work one st in moss st, P2, patt 26 sts as 1st row of trailing leaves panel, 12 sts as 1st row of cable panel, 26 sts as 1st row of trailing leaves panel, P2, work one st in moss st.
2nd row Work one st in moss st, K2, patt 26 sts as 2nd row of trailing leaves panel, 12 sts as 2nd row of cable panel, 26 sts as 2nd row of trailing leaves panel, K2, work one st in moss st.
Cont in patt as set, inc one st at each end of next and every foll 3rd row until there are 128 sts, working extra sts in moss st. Cont without shaping until sleeve measures 39.5[39.5:40.5]cm (15½[15½:16]in) from beg, ending with a WS row.

88

Design Nº 18

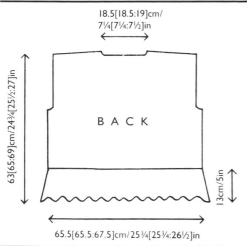

18.5[18.5:19]cm/
7¼[7¼:7½]in

63[65:69]cm/24¾[25½:27]in

BACK

13cm/5in

65.5[65.5:67.5]cm/25¾[25¾:26½]in

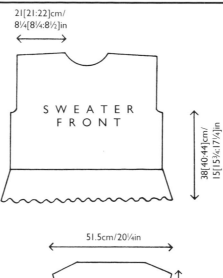

21[21:22]cm/
8¼[8¼:8½]in

SWEATER FRONT

38[40:44]cm/
15[15¾:17¼]in

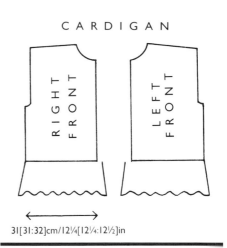

CARDIGAN

RIGHT FRONT   **LEFT FRONT**

31[31:32]cm/12¼[12¼:12½]in

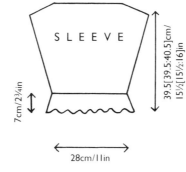

51.5cm/20¼in

SLEEVE

7cm/2¾in

39.5[39.5:40.5]cm/15½[15½:16]in

28cm/11in

Shape armhole

Keeping patt correct, cast off 3 sts at beg of next and foll alt row. 72[72:74] sts. Cont without shaping until armhole measures 21cm (8¼in) from beg, ending at front edge.

Shape neck

Cast off at beg of next and foll alt rows 6 sts once, 5 sts once, 4 sts once, 2 sts once and one st twice. 53[53:55] sts. Cont without shaping until Front matches Back to shoulder, ending at armhole edge.

Shape shoulder

Cast off 26[26:27] sts at beg of next row. Work one row. Cast off rem 27[27:28] sts.

RIGHT FRONT

Work as given for Left Front, but reversing position of pocket lining and setting patt as foll:

1st row (WS) For last size only work 2 sts in moss st, then for all sizes (patt 12 sts as 1st row of cable panel, 26 sts as 1st row of trailing leaves panel) twice, P2, turn and sl last 6 sts on to a safety-pin for Buttonhole Band. 78[78:80] sts.

SLEEVES

Work as given for Sleeves of Sweater, noting the bracketed exception.

POCKET TOPS

Using 4mm (US6) needles and with RS of work facing, sl 30 sts on holder on to left-hand needle. Join in yarn and work 5 rows in moss st. Cast off in patt.

BUTTON BAND

Using 3¼mm (US3) needles and with RS of work facing, sl Button Band sts on to left-hand needle. Join in yarn, inc in first st, work in moss st to end. 7 sts. Cont in moss st until band, when slightly stretched, fits up Left Front edge to neck, ending with a WS row. Cut off yarn. Leave sts on a safety-pin. Mark position of 6 buttons with pins, the first to come 1cm (½in) above ruffle and the last 1cm (½in) down from neck edge, with the

others evenly spaced between. Sew band in position.

BUTTONHOLE BAND

Using 3¼mm (US3) needles and with WS of work facing, sl Buttonhole Band sts on to left-hand needle. Join in yarn, inc in first st, work in moss st to end. 7 sts. Cont as given for

Button Band, but do not cut off yarn and making buttonholes as markers are reached as foll:
Buttonhole row (RS) Patt 3 sts, yo, K2 tog, patt 2.
Sew band in position.

COLLAR

Join shoulder seams.
Using 3¼mm (US3) needles and with RS of work facing, patt across 7 sts of Buttonhole Band, pick up and K 29 sts up right front neck, K across 16[46:47] back neck sts, pick up and K 29 sts down left front neck and patt across 7 sts of Button Band. 118[118:119] sts. Work 10cm (4in) in moss st. Cast off in patt.

TO MAKE UP

Sew down pocket linings on WS of work and ends of pocket tops on RS. Set in sleeves. Join side and sleeve seams. Sew on buttons.

Design Nº 19

CORAL Reef

Soft cotton yarn used double makes a striking fabric for this picture sweater in warm tones of navy and ecru. The multi-size instructions ensure that there is a version to fit all members of the family.

SIZES

To fit chest 56-61[66-71:76-81:102:107:112]cm (22-24[26-28:30-32:40:42:44]in)
Actual size 68[84:92:114:121:128]cm (26½[33:36:45:47½:50]in)
Length to shoulder 38.5[45:51:64:67:70]cm (15[17¾:20:25:26½:27½]in)
Sleeve seam 23[26:29.5:50:50:51]cm (9[10¼:11½:19½:19½:20]in)
Figures in square brackets [] refer to larger sizes; where there is only one set of figures, it applies to all sizes

MATERIALS

4[5:6:14:14:15] × 50g balls of Rowan Sea Breeze in main colour A (Turkish Plum 529)
2[2:3:7:7:8] balls in colour B (Ecru 522)
Note that yarn is used double throughout
Pair each of 3¼mm (US3) and 4mm (US6) knitting needles

TENSION

23 sts and 28 rows to 10cm (4in) over intarsia patt using 4mm (US6) needles

BACK

Using 3¼mm (US3) needles and A, cast on 68[84:94:100:104:106] sts. Work 5[6:6:7:7:7]cm (2[2½:2½:2¾:2¾:2¾]in) in K1, P1 rib, ending with a RS row.
Next row Rib 6[3:8:4:6:7], inc in next st, (rib 5[6:6:9:9:9], inc in next st) to last 7[3:8:5:7:8] sts, rib to end.

78[96:106:110:114:116] sts.
Change to 4mm (US6) needles.
Beg with a K row, cont in st st and patt from Chart 3[3:3:1:1:1], starting at Chart row 25[9:1:17:9:1]. Read odd-numbered (K) rows from right to left and even-numbered (P) rows from left to right. Strand colour not in use loosely across WS of work where appropriate or use small, separate balls of yarn for individual motifs.

Last 3 sizes only
Work 4 rows. Inc one st at each end of next and every foll 4th row until there are 132[140:148] sts.
All sizes
Cont in patt without shaping until Chart row 74[68:70:106:106:106] has been completed, so ending with a P row.

Shape armholes
Cast off 2[3:3:3:3:3] sts at beg of next 2 rows, 2 sts at beg of foll 2 rows and one st at beg of next 0[0:0:2:2:2] rows.
70[86:96:120:128:136] sts. *

Cont without shaping until Chart row 118[118:126:176:176:176] has been completed, so ending with a P row.

Shape shoulders and back neck
Next row Cast off 9[13:15:20:22:25] sts, patt until there are 9[12:15:20:22:23] sts on right-hand needle, turn.
Work one row. Cast off rem 9[12:15:20:22:23] sts.
With RS of work facing, sl centre 34[36:36:40:40:40] sts on to a holder, rejoin yarn to next st and patt to end.
Next row Cast off 9[13:15:20:22:25] sts, patt to end.
Work one row. Cast off rem 9[12:15:20:22:23] sts.

Folklore is passed down from father to son. Here Mark tells William fascinating tales of the South Seas. Their 'Coral Reef' sweaters, dominated by imposing galleons in full sail and other imagery from the Pacific, add credence to the stories.

Design Nº 19

CHART 1

□ A

☒ B

SLEEVE

4TH SIZE BACK

5TH SIZE BACK

6TH SIZE BACK

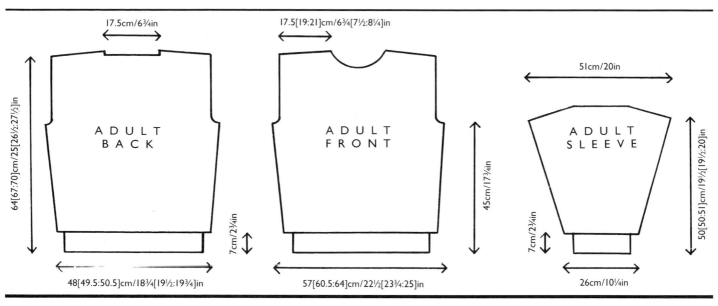

17.5cm/6¾in

17.5[19:21]cm/6¾[7½:8¼]in

51cm/20in

64[67:70]cm/25[25:26½:27½]in

ADULT
BACK

ADULT
FRONT

ADULT
SLEEVE

45cm/17¾in

50[50:51]cm/19½[19½:20]in

7cm/2¾in

7cm/2¾in

48[49.5:50.5]cm/18¾[19½:19¾]in

57[60.5:64]cm/22½[23¾:25]in

26cm/10¼in

FRONT

Work as given for Back to *.
Cont without shaping until Chart row
104[104:112:162:162:162] has been
completed, so ending with a P row.

Shape neck

Next row Patt 28[36:41:52:56:60] sts, turn
and leave rem sts on a spare needle.
Complete left side of neck first.
Cast off at beg of next and foll alt rows
4[4:4:5:5:5] sts once, 3 sts once, 2 sts once
and one st 1[2:2:2:2:2] times.
18[25:30:40:44:48] sts. Cont without shaping
until Chart row 118[118:126:176:176:176]
(row 119[119:127:177:177:177] for other side
of neck) has been completed, so ending at
armhole edge.

Shape shoulder

Cast off 9[13:15:20:22:25] sts at beg of next
row. Work one row. Cast off rem
9[12:15:20:22:23] sts.
With RS of work facing, sl centre
14[14:14:16:16:16] sts on to a holder, rejoin
yarn to next st and patt to end. Work one
row, then complete as given for other side of
neck, noting the bracketed exception.

SLEEVES

Using 3¼mm (US3) needles and A, cast on
32[40:42:48:48:48] sts. Work 5[6:6:7:7:7]cm
(2[2½:2½:2¾:2¾:2¾]in) in K1, P1 rib,
ending with a RS row.

CHART 2

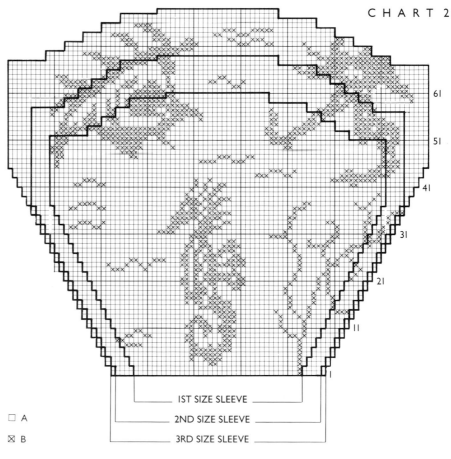

61

51

41

31

21

11

1

□ A

☒ B

1ST SIZE SLEEVE

2ND SIZE SLEEVE

3RD SIZE SLEEVE

'*The South Seas and the tales that come from there evoke memories of
childhood adventure for me – Treasure Island, Captain Hook and shipwrecks
galore. The galleon with its billowing sails makes a magnificent centrepiece
for this design. I have also included exotic flowers and sea life from the
Pacific. To maximize the impact of this busy design, it is knitted in two
colours only.*'

Design N.º 19

CHART 3

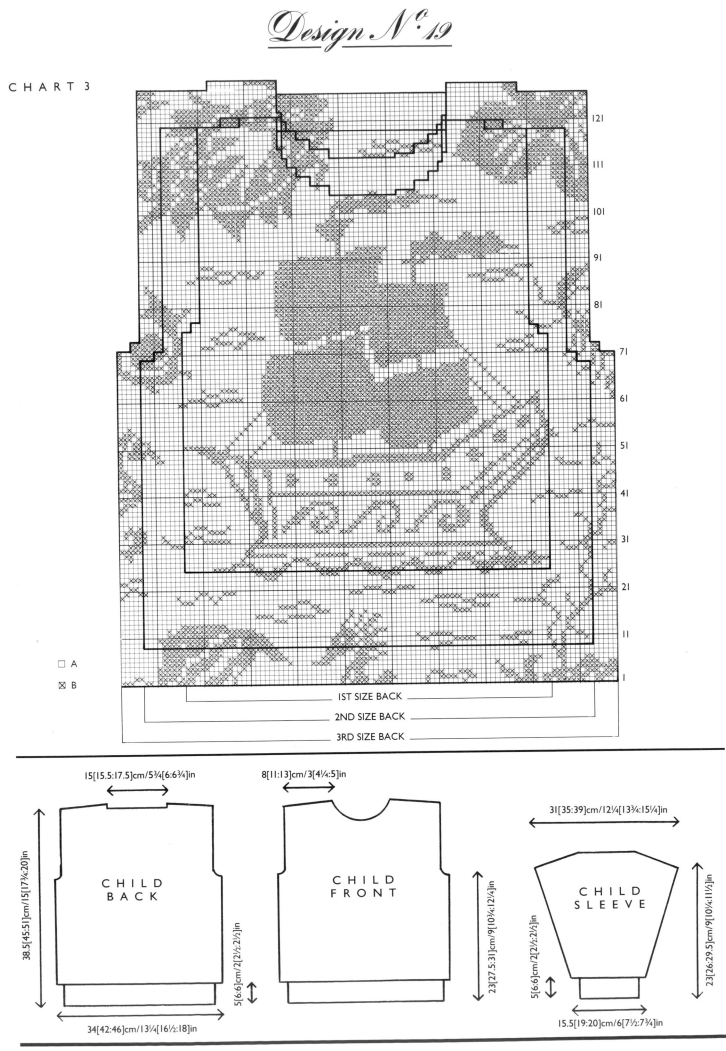

□ A
⊠ B

1ST SIZE BACK
2ND SIZE BACK
3RD SIZE BACK

15[15.5:17.5]cm/5¾[6:6¾]in

8[11:13]cm/3[4¼:5]in

31[35:39]cm/12¼[13¾:15¼]in

38.5[45:51]cm/15[17¾:20]in

CHILD
BACK

5[6:6]cm/2[2½:2½]in

CHILD
FRONT

23[27.5:31]cm/9[10¾:12¼]in

CHILD
SLEEVE

5[6:6]cm/2[2½:2½]in

23[26:29.5]cm/9[10¼:11½]in

34[42:46]cm/13¼[16½:18]in

15.5[19:20]cm/6[7½:7¾]in

Design Nᵒ 19

K15[15:16:16:16:16] sts down left front neck, K across 14[14:14:16:16:16] sts on holder, pick up and K15[15:16:16:16:16] sts up right front neck, one st down right back neck, K across 34[36:36:40:40:40] sts on holder and pick up and K one st up left back neck. 80[82:84:90:90:90] sts.
Work 6cm (2½in) in K1, P1 rib. Cast off loosely in rib.

TO MAKE UP

Press on WS of work using a warm iron over a damp cloth. Join left shoulder and neckband seam. Fold neckband in half to inside and slip stitch in position. Set in sleeves. Join side and sleeve seams. Press seams.

William plays on the shore protected from the cool breeze by his seascape sweater. 'Coral Reef' is worked in cotton yarn used double so that it knits up rapidly; in popular navy and ecru it is a perfect sweater for nautical pursuits in unpredictable weather.

Next row Rib 3[6:7:2:2:2], inc in next st, (rib 7[8:8:3:3:3], inc in next st) to last 4[6:7:1:1:1] sts, rib to end. 36[44:46:60:60:60] sts.
Beg with a K row, cont in st st and patt from Chart 2[2:2:1:1:1], inc one st at each end of 3rd[3rd:3rd:4th:4th:4th] and every foll alt[alt:alt:3rd:3rd:3rd] row until there are 72[80:90:96:96:96] sts.

Last 3 sizes only
Now inc one st at each end of every foll 4th row until there are 118 sts.

All sizes
Cont without shaping until Chart row 50[56:66:120:120:124] has been completed, so ending with a P row.

Shape top
Cast off at beg of next and foll alt rows 8[7:8:8:8:8] sts twice, 3[3:4:4:4:4] sts 6[8:8:10:10:10] times and 8 sts twice. Cast off rem 22[26:26:46:46:46] sts.

NECKBAND

Join right shoulder seam.
Using 3¼mm (US3) needles, A and with RS of work facing, pick up and

Design Nº 20
Peony

Here a cotton sweater has been used as a backdrop for a dramatic monochrome floral design. Instead of ribbed hems, the lower edges, cuffs and neck are neatened with a stocking stitch hem and trimmed with optional crochet bobbles.

SIZES

To fit bust 87-91[96-102:107-112]cm (34-36[38-40:42-44]in)
Actual size 122[127:134]cm (48[50:53]in)
Length to shoulder 66[68.5:71.5]cm (26[27:28¼]in)
Sleeve seam 37[38.5:40]cm (14½[15:15¾]in)
Figures in square brackets [] refer to larger sizes; where there is only one set of figures, it applies to all sizes.

MATERIALS

16[17:18] × 50g balls of Rowan Handknit DK Cotton in main colour A (Black 252)
10[11:11] balls in colour B (Ecru 251)
Pair of 4mm (US6) knitting needles
3.50mm (US E/4) crochet hook

TENSION

22 sts and 28 rows to 10 cm (4in) over intarsia patt using 4mm (US6) needles

BACK

Using 4mm (US6) needles and A, cast on 116[122:130] sts. Beg with a K row, cont in st st and patt from Chart, starting at row 17[9:1]. Read odd-numbered (K) rows from right to left and even-numbered (P) rows from left to right. Strand colour not in use loosely across WS of work where appropriate or use small, separate balls of yarn for individual motifs.
Work 10 rows. Inc one st at each end of next and every foll 10th row until there are 134[140:148] sts. Cont without shaping until Chart row 132 has been completed, so ending with a P row.

A dramatic example of Japanese floral geometry in the shape of this sweater worn by Monica.

Shape armholes

Cast off 3 sts at beg of next 2 rows and 2 sts at beg of foll 2 rows. 124[130:138] sts.*
Cont without shaping until Chart row 200 has been completed, so ending with a P row.

Shape shoulders and back neck

Next row Cast off 17[20:24] sts, K until there are 23 sts on right-hand needle, turn and complete right side of neck first.
Work one row.
Cast off rem 23 sts.
With RS of work facing, sl centre 44 sts on to a holder, rejoin yarn to next st and patt to end.
Next row Cast off 17[20:24] sts, patt to end.
Work one row. Cast off rem 23 sts.

FRONT

Work as given for Back to *.
Cont without shaping until Chart row 184 has been completed, so ending with a P row.

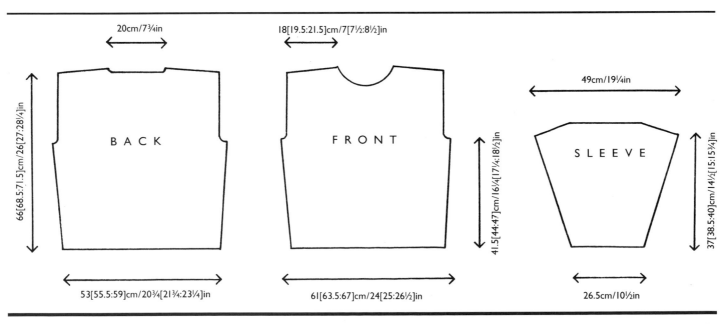

BACK — 20cm/7¾in — 66[68.5:71.5]cm/26[27:28¼]in — 53[55.5:59]cm/20¾[21¾:23¼]in

FRONT — 18[19.5:21.5]cm/7[7½:8½]in — 41.5[44:47]cm/16¼[17¼:18½]in — 61[63.5:67]cm/24[25:26½]in

SLEEVE — 49cm/19¼in — 37[38.5:40]cm/14½[15:15¾]in — 26.5cm/10½in

Design Nº 20

Shape neck

Next row Patt 54[57:61] sts, turn and leave rem sts on a spare needle.
Complete left side of neck first. Cast off at beg of next and foll alt rows 6 sts once, 4 sts once, 2 sts once and one st twice. 40[43:47] sts. Cont without shaping until Chart row 200 (row 201 for other side of neck) has been completed, so ending at armhole edge.

Shape shoulder

Cast off 17[20:24] sts at beg of next row. Work one row. Cast off rem 23 sts.
With RS of work facing, sl centre 16 sts on to a holder, rejoin yarn to next st and patt to end. Work one row. Complete as given for other side of neck, noting the bracketed exception.

SLEEVES

Using 4mm (US6) needles and A, cast on 58 sts. Beg with a K row, cont in st st and patt from Chart, inc one st at each end of 5th and every foll 4th row until there are 108 sts. Cont without shaping until Chart row 104[108:112] has been completed, so ending with a P row.

Shape top

Cast off 6 sts at beg of next 2 rows, 5 sts at beg of foll 8 rows and 9 sts at beg of next 2 rows. Cast off rem 38 sts.

NECK FACING

Join right shoulder seam.
Using 4mm (US6) needles, A and with RS of work facing, pick up and K24 sts down left front neck, K across 16 sts on holder, pick up and K 24 sts up right front neck, one st from right back neck, K across 44 sts on holder and pick up and K one st up left back neck. 110 sts.
Next 2 rows K to end.
Next row P to end.
Next row K11, pick up loop lying between needles and K tbl – called make 1 (M1), (K4, M1) 3 times, K18, (M1, K4) 3 times, M1, K11, (M1, K8) twice, M1, K14, (M1, K8) twice. 123 sts.
Cont in st st until facing measures 5 cm (2in) from beg, ending with a P row. Cast off.

HEM BORDERS

Join left shoulder and facing seam.

Back

Using 4mm (US6) needles, A and with RS of work facing, K up 116[122:130] sts along lower edge. K one row.
Next row (dec row) (K8, K2 tog) to last 6[2:0] sts, K6[2:0]. 105[110:117] sts. Work 12 more rows in st st. Cast off.

Front

Work as given for Back.

Sleeves

Work as given for Back, but picking up 58 sts and with dec row as foll:
Dec row K8, (K2 tog, K8) to end. 53 sts.

BOBBLES

Using 3.50mm (US E/4) crochet hook and A, make 2ch.
1st round Work 8dc into 2nd ch from hook. Join with a ss into first dc.
2nd round Work 2dc into each dc to end. 16dc.

3rd round (Miss 1dc, 1dc into next dc) to end. 8dc.
Cut off yarn, leaving a long end.
Thread yarn through each of 8 sts and draw tight to close bobble.
Fasten off and secure yarn, leaving a long end for sewing on to garment.
Make approximately 25 bobbles in A and 25 in B.

TO MAKE UP

Press on WS of work using a warm iron over a damp cloth. Set in sleeves. Join side and sleeve seams. Fold facing at neck and borders at hem and sleeve edges to inside and slip stitch in position.
Press seams.
Sew on bobbles to hem, cuff and neck edges at regular intervals apart – about 4 cm (1½in).

'The Japanese have perfected the art of 'minimalism' in fabric printing and woodcuts, yet there is often such balance to a design that it creates a rich, harmonious quality. With 'Peony' I wanted to show a two-colour floral pattern that was strong over a large expanse of fabric, but quite easy to knit. The bobble trimmings are an added touch to echo the shape of the flower buds.'

Boomerang

A crew neck child's sweater knitted in a lightweight double knitting that is warm without being too bulky. Animal motifs are worked into a monochrome intarsia pattern.

SIZES

To fit 61-66[71-76]cm (24-26[28-30]in) chest
Actual size 80[91]cm (31½[35¾]in)
Length to shoulder 49[51]cm (19¼[20]in)
Sleeve seam 29[31]cm (11½[12¼]in)
Figures in square brackets [] refer to larger size; where there is only one set of figures, it applies to both sizes

MATERIALS

12[14] × 25g hanks of Rowan Lightweight DK in main colour A (black 62)
4[5] hanks in contrast colour B (ecru 2)
Pair each of 3mm (US3) and 3¾mm (US5) knitting needles

TENSION

25 sts and 28 rows to 10cm (4in) over intarsia patt using 3¾mm (US5) needles

BACK

Using 3mm (US3) needles and A, cast on 96[106] sts. Work 6cm (2½in) in K1, P1 rib.
Change to 3¾mm (US5) needles.
Beg with a K row, cont in st st, and patt from Chart, starting at row 7[1]. Strand colour not in use loosely across back of work where appropriate or use small, separate balls of yarn for individual motifs. Work 14[10] rows, then inc one st at each end of next and every foll 20th[10th] row until there are 100[114] sts. Cont without shaping until Chart row 76 has been completed, so ending with a P row.

Cousins Thomas and William are searching for dragons. This might be child's play, but Thomas (right) makes sure that he is suitably dressed in 'Boomerang' – a black sweater with white primitive animal motifs. William (left) is wearing 'Bright Cree' (page 121).

Shape armholes
Cast off 3 sts at beg of next 2 rows and 2 sts at beg of foll 2 rows. 90[104] sts. *
Cont without shaping until Chart row 126 has been completed, so ending with a P row.

Shape shoulders and back neck
Next row Cast off 8[15] sts, K until there are 17 sts on right hand needle, turn and complete right side of neck first.
Work one row. Cast off rem 17 sts.
With RS of work facing, sl centre 40 sts on to a holder for back neck, rejoin yarn to rem sts and patt to end.
Next row Cast off 8[15] sts, patt to end.
Work one row.
Cast off rem 17 sts.

FRONT

Work as given for Back to *.
Cont without shaping until Chart row 114 has been completed, so ending with a P row.

Shape neck
Next row Patt 34[41] sts, turn and leave rem sts on a spare needle.
Complete left side of neck first. ** Cast off 4 sts at beg of next row, 3 sts at beg of foll alt row and one st at beg of next 2 alt rows. 25[32] sts. Cont without shaping until Chart row 126 (row 127 for other side of neck) has been completed, so ending at armhole edge.

Shape shoulder
Cast off 8[15] sts at beg of next row. Work one row. Cast off rem 17 sts.
With RS of work facing, sl centre 22 sts on to a holder, rejoin yarn to rem sts and patt to end. Work one row, then complete as given for other side of neck from ** to end, noting the bracketed exception.

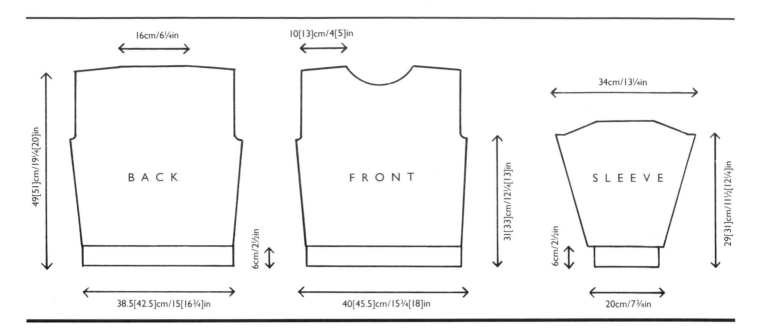

16cm/6¼in

10[13]cm/4[5]in

34cm/13¼in

49[51]cm/19¼[20]in

BACK

6cm/2½in

FRONT

31[33]cm/12¼[13]in

SLEEVE

29[31]cm/11½[12¼]in

6cm/2½in

38.5[42.5]cm/15[16¾]in

40[45.5]cm/15¾[18]in

20cm/7¾in

SLEEVES

Using 3mm (US3) needles and A, cast on 44[46] sts. Work 6cm (2½in) in K1, P1 rib.
Next row Rib 4[6], inc in next st, (rib 6[10], inc in next st) to last 4[6] sts, rib to end. 50 sts.
Change to 3¾mm (US5) needles.
Beg with a K row, cont in st st and patt from Chart starting at row 7. Inc one st at each end of 4th and every foll 3rd row until there are 86 sts. Cont without shaping until Chart row 70[76] has been completed, so ending with a P row.

Shape top
Cast off 4 sts at beg of every row until 38 sts rem. Cast off.

NECKBAND

Join right shoulder seam.
Using 3mm (US3) needles, A and with RS of work facing, pick up and K17 sts down left front neck, K across centre 22 sts on holder, pick up and K17 sts up right front neck, one st from right back neck, K across 40 back neck sts on holder and pick up and K one st from left back neck. 98 sts.
Work 6cm (2½in) in K1, P1 rib. Cast off loosely in rib.

TO MAKE UP

Press on WS using a warm iron over a damp cloth. Join left shoulder and neckband seam. Fold neckband in half to WS and slip stitch in position. Set in sleeves. Join side and sleeve seams. Press seams.

The afternoon shadows provide a striking backdrop for three designs in black and white. Monica (left) wears a bobble-trimmed sweater, 'Peony' (page 97), Thomas (standing) is in 'Boomerang' and Richard (right) wears an 'Ibo' cardigan (page 107).

Design № 21

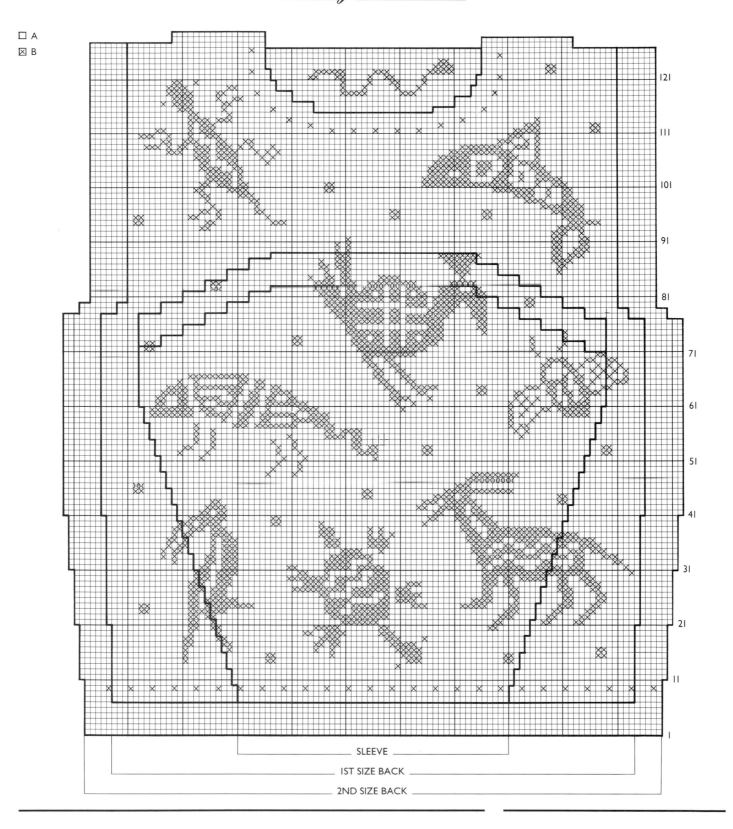

□ A
☒ B

SLEEVE

IST SIZE BACK

2ND SIZE BACK

'I am lucky in that although I am no longer in London, Brighton – where I now live – is closely associated with the 'arts' that I appreciate. In particular I remember an exhibition of Aboriginal Art and Bark Painting at Brighton Museum.

The primitive two-colour drawings were fascinating as they seemed to be free of all outside influences. Certain elements were so child-like and naive that I immediately linked them to some children's designs that I was working on at the time.'

Overleaf *Three generations pose together in a family group that demonstrates Annabel's philosophy that one is never too young or too old to wear one of her designs. In this positive and negative collection Mark (seated – left) wears 'Coral Reef' (page 91), Brigit (centre) is in an 'Ibo' cardigan (page 107) and Annabel (right) models 'Peony' (page 97).*

Ibo

Available as a sweater or cardigan with useful pockets, this striking design with an Aboriginal influence is in stocking stitch and Rowan DK Cotton.

SIZES

To fit chest 102-107[112-117:117-122]cm (40-42[44-46:46-48]in)
Actual size 128[135:141]cm (50[53:55½]in)
Length to shoulder 68[70:73]cm (26¾[27½:28¾]in)
Sleeve seam 50.5[50.5:53]cm (19¾[19¾:20¾]in)
Figures in square brackets [] refer to larger sizes; where there is only one set of figures, it applies to all sizes

MATERIALS

18[18:19] × 50g balls of Rowan DK Cotton in main colour A (Black 252)
6[6:7] balls in colour B (Ecru 251)
Pair each of 3¼mm (US3) and 4mm (US6) knitting needles
3¼mm (US3) circular knitting needle, long length for Cardigan
5 buttons for Cardigan

TENSION

21 sts and 25.5 rows to 10cm (4in) over patt using 4mm (US6) needles

Richard soaks up the evening sun in this powerful cardigan with mystical motifs on the fronts and an entirely different diamond-shaped pattern on the sleeves.

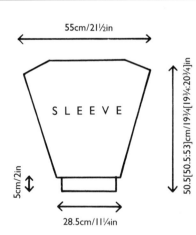

55cm/21½in

SLEEVE

50.5[50.5:53]cm/19¾[19¾:20¾]in

5cm/2in

28.5cm/11¼in

SWEATER

BACK

Using 3¼mm (US3) needles and A, cast on 96[100:104] sts. Join in B and work in 2-colour rib, carrying yarn not in use loosely across WS of work.
1st row (RS) (Using A, P1, using B, K1) to end.
2nd row (Using B, P1, using A, K1) to end.
Rep these 2 rows until work measures 5cm (2in) from beg, ending with a WS row.
Next row Using A, (P1, K1) to end.
Next row Using A, P10[4:2], inc in next st, (P3, inc in next st) to last 9[3:1] sts, P to end. 116[124:130] sts.
Change to 4mm (US6) needles.
Beg with a K row, cont in st st and patt from Chart, starting at row 15[9:1]. Read odd-numbered (K) rows from right to left and even-numbered (P) rows from left to right.
Strand colour not in use loosely across WS of work where appropriate or use small, separate balls of yarn for individual motifs.
Work 8[10:10] rows. Inc one st at each end of next and every foll 8th[10th:10th] row until

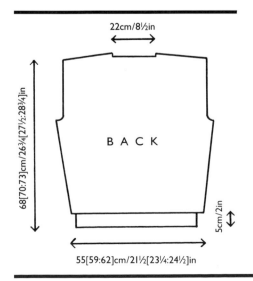

22cm/8½in

BACK

68[70:73]cm/26¾[27½:28¾]in

5cm/2in

55[59:62]cm/21½[23¼:24½]in

18[20:21.5]cm/7[7¾:8½]in

SWEATER FRONT

40[42.5:45.5]cm/15¾[16¾:17¾]in

64[67.5:70.5]cm/25[26½:27¾]in

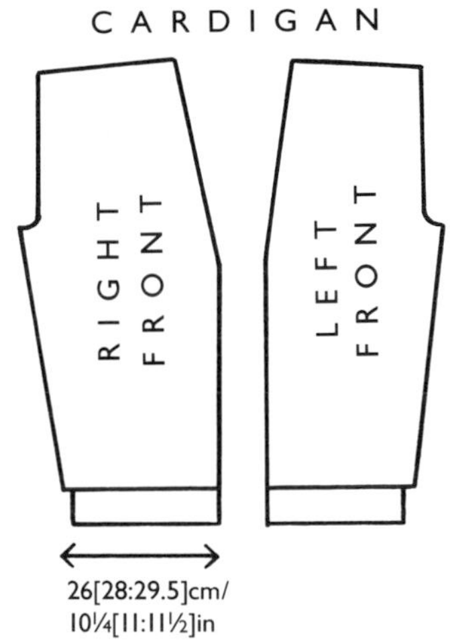

CARDIGAN

RIGHT FRONT

LEFT FRONT

26[28:29.5]cm/ 10¼[11:11½]in

Design Nº 22

□ A
⊠ B

171
161
151
141
131
121
111
101
91
81
71
61
51
41
31
21
11
1

1ST SIZE RIGHT FRONT — 1ST SIZE LEFT FRONT
1ST SIZE BACK
2ND SIZE RIGHT FRONT — 2ND SIZE LEFT FRONT
2ND SIZE BACK
3RD SIZE RIGHT FRONT — 3RD SIZE LEFT FRONT
3RD SIZE BACK

Design N° 22

'My cousin, who lives in Australia, frequently sends me postcards and leaflets of Aboriginal art which are great sources of reference for my work. The images are often so powerful that they look best shown as strong two-colour designs. In 'Ibo' I have combined animal and mythical folklore with geometric symbols, framing the resulting picture with a striped border.'

there are 134[142:148] sts. Cont without shaping until Chart row 104 has been completed, so ending with a P row.

Shape armholes

Cast off 3 sts at beg of next 2 rows, 2 sts at beg of foll 2 rows and one st at beg of next 2 rows. 122[130:136] sts. *
Cont without shaping until Chart row 174 has been completed, so ending with a P row.

Shape shoulders and back neck

Next row Cast off 14[18:21] sts, K until there are 24 sts on right-hand needle, turn.
Work one row. Cast off rem 24 sts.
With RS of work facing, sl centre 46 sts on to a holder, rejoin yarn to next st and K to end.
Next row Cast off 14[18:21] sts, P to end.
Work one row. Cast off rem 24 sts.

FRONT

Work as given for Back to *.
Cont without shaping until Chart row 156 has been completed, so ending with a P row.

Shape neck

Next row K52[56:59], turn and leave rem sts on a spare needle.
Complete left side of neck first.
Cast off at beg of next and foll alt rows 5 sts once, 4 sts once, 2 sts twice and one st once. 38[42:45] sts.
Cont without shaping until Chart row 174 (row 175 for other side of neck) has been completed, so ending at armhole edge.

Shape shoulder

Cast off 14[18:21] sts at beg of next row.
Work one row. Cast off rem 24 sts.
With RS of work facing, sl centre 18 sts on to a holder, rejoin yarn to next st and K to end.
Work one row, then complete as given for other side of neck, noting the bracketed exception.

SLEEVES

Using 3¼mm (US3) needles and A, cast on 50 sts. Work 5cm (2in) in 2-colour rib as given for Back welt, ending with a WS row.
Next row Using A, (P1, K1) to end.
Next row Using A, P2, inc in next st, (P4, inc in next st) to last 2 sts, P2. 60 sts.
Change to 4mm (US6) needles.
Beg with a K row, cont in st st and patt from Chart, inc one st at each end of 5th and every foll 4th row until there are 116 sts. Cont without shaping until Chart row 116[116:122] has been completed, so ending with a P row.

Shape top

Cast off at beg of next and foll rows 6 sts twice, 4 sts 10 times and 12 sts twice. Cast off rem 40 sts.

NECKBAND

Join right shoulder seam.
Using 3¼mm (US3) needles, A and with RS of work facing, pick up and K24 sts down left front neck, K across 18 sts on holder, pick up and K24 sts up right front neck, one st down right back neck, K across 46 sts on holder and pick up and K one st up left back neck. 114 sts.
Next row (WS) (P1, K1) to end.
Join in B and work in 2-colour rib as before until neckband measures 3cm (1¼in) from beg, ending with a RS row. Cut off B.
Next row Using A, rib to end.
Cast off in rib.

TO MAKE UP

Press on WS of work using a warm iron over a damp cloth. Join left shoulder and neckband seam. Set in sleeves. Join side and sleeve seams. Press seams.

CARDIGAN

BACK

Work as given for Back of Sweater.

POCKET LININGS
(make 2)

Using 4mm (US6) needles and A, cast on 28 sts. Beg with a K row, work 38 rows in st st. Cut off yarn. Leave sts on a holder.

LEFT FRONT

Using 3¼mm (US3) needles and A, cast on 46[48:50] sts. Work 5cm (2in) in 2-colour rib as given for Back welt, ending with a WS row.
Next row Using A, (P1, K1) to end.
Next row Using A, P3[4:3], inc in next st, (P4[3:3], inc in next st) to last 2[3:2] sts, P to end. 55[59:62] sts.
Change to 4mm (US6) needles.
Beg with a K row, cont in st st and patt from Chart, starting at row 15[9:1]. Work 8[10:10] rows. Inc one st at beg (read 'end' here for Right Front) of next and every foll 8th[10th:10th] row until Chart row 54 has been completed.

Place pocket
Next row Patt 8[12:16] sts (inc in first st for 1st size only), sl next 28 sts on to a holder, K across 28 sts of first pocket lining, patt to end.
Cont in patt from Chart, inc as before, until Chart row 89 (row 88 for Right Front) has been completed, so ending at front edge.

Shape front edge

Cont to inc at side edge as indicated, *at the same time* dec one st at front edge at beg of next and every foll 4th row until Chart row 104 (row 105 for Right Front) has been completed, so ending at side edge.

Shape armhole

Cont to dec at front edge as before, cast off 3 sts at beg of next row, 2 sts at beg of foll alt row and one st at beg of next alt row.

Design Nº 22

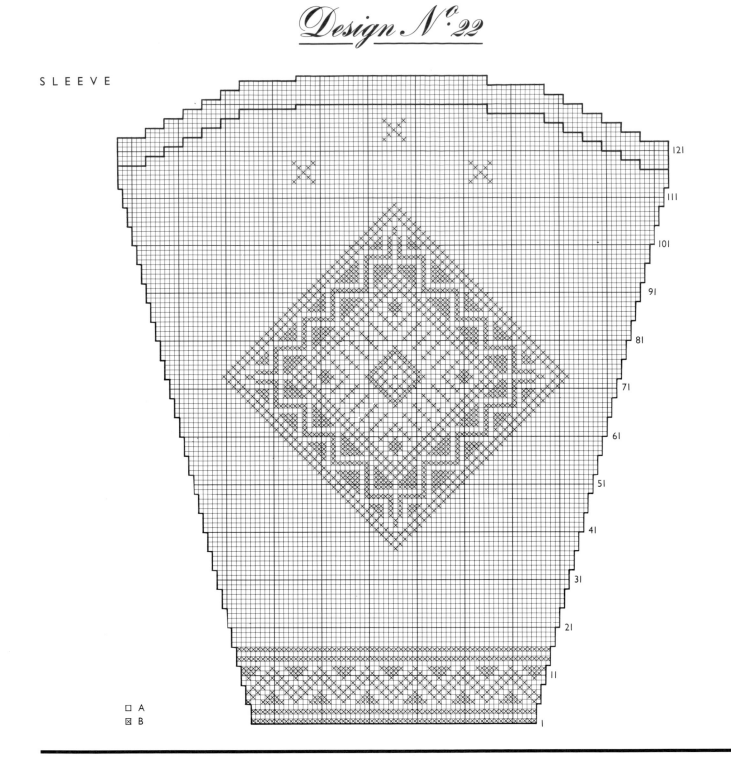

□ A
⊠ B

53[57:60] sts. (52[56:59] sts for Right Front.)
Keeping armhole edge straight, cont to dec at
front edge only until 38[42:45] sts rem. Cont
without shaping until Chart row 174 (row
175 for Right Front) has been completed, so
ending at armhole edge.

Shape shoulder
Cast off 14[18:21] sts at beg of next row.
Work one row. Cast off rem 24 sts.

RIGHT FRONT

Work as given for Left Front, following the
appropriate Chart and noting the bracketed
exceptions. Also place pocket as foll:
Chart row 55 Patt 23 sts, sl next 28 sts on to
a holder, K across sts of second pocket lining,
patt to end (inc in last st for 1st size only).

SLEEVES

Work as given for Sleeves of Sweater.

FRONT BAND

Join shoulder seams.
Using 3¼mm (US3) circular needle, A and
with RS of work facing, beg at lower edge of
right front and pick up and K11 sts along rib,
70[74:81] sts to start of shaping, 71 sts to
shoulder, one st down right back neck, K
across back neck sts on holder, pick up and K
one st up left back neck, 71 sts down left
front neck to start of shaping, 70[74:81] sts
down left front to rib and 11 sts along rib.
352[360:374] sts.
Join in B and work in 2-colour rib as foll:
Next row (WS) (Using B, P1, using A, K1) to
end.
Next row (buttonhole row) Keeping colours

correct, rib 271[275:284], yo, work 2 tog, (rib
17[18:19], yo, work 2 tog) 4 times, rib 3[3:4].
Work 5 more rows in rib as set. Cast off in
rib using A only.

POCKET TOPS

Using 4mm (US6) needles, A and with RS of
work facing, P across 28 sts on holder to
mark foldline.
Beg with a P row, work 2cm (¾in) in st st.
Cast off.

TO MAKE UP

Press on WS of work using a warm iron over
a damp cloth. Turn pocket tops to inside at
foldline and slip stitch in position. Slip stitch
pocket linings in position on WS of work. Set
in sleeves. Join side and sleeve seams. Press
seams. Sew on buttons.

Santos

A crew neck man's sweater knitted in Rowan DK Cotton. Bright rectangles of geometric patterns are isolated against a broad grid of vivid red background in stocking stitch.

SIZES

To fit chest 102[107:112]cm (40[42:44]in)
Actual size 128[136:142]cm (50[53½:56]in)
Length to shoulder 69[71:74]cm
(27[28:29]in)
Sleeve seam 53[53:54.5]cm
(20¾[20¾:21½]in)
Figures in square brackets [] refer to larger sizes; where there is only one set of figures, it applies to all sizes

MATERIALS

17[17:18] × 50g balls of Rowan DK Cotton in main colour A (Cherry 298)
2 balls in colour B (Black 252)
2 balls in colour C (Port 245)
3 balls in colour D (China Blue 267)
2 balls in colour E (Bayou 279)
2 balls in colour F (Mango 262)
2 balls in colour G (Royal 294)
2 balls in colour H (Violet 256)
1 ball in colour I (Mustard 246)
Pair each of 3¼mm (US3) and 4mm (US6) knitting needles

TENSION

20 sts and 28 rows to 10cm (4in) over st st using 4mm (US6) needles

BACK

Using 3¼mm (US3) needles and A, cast on 96[100:104] sts. Work 6cm (2½in) in K1, P1 rib, ending with a RS row.
Next row Rib 8[7:4], inc in next st, (rib 5[4:4], inc in next st) to last 9[7:4] sts, rib to end. 110[118:124] sts.
Change to 4mm (US6) needles.
Beg with a K row, cont in st st and patt from Chart, starting at row 15[9:1]. Read odd-numbered (K) rows from right to left and even-numbered (P) rows from left to right.
Strand colour not in use loosely across WS of work where appropriate or use, small separate balls of yarn for individual motifs.
Work 10[10:12] rows. Inc one st at each end of next and every foll 10th[10th:12th] row

until there are 128[136:142] sts. Cont without shaping until Chart row 118 has been completed, so ending with a P row.

Shape armholes

Cast off 3 sts at beg of next 2 rows, 2 sts at beg of foll 2 rows and one st at beg of next 2 rows. 116[124:130] sts. *
Cont without shaping until Chart row 190 has been completed, so ending with a P row.

Shape shoulders and back neck

Next row Cast off 19[21:23] sts, K until there are 19[21:22] sts on right-hand needle, turn. Work one row. Cast off rem 19[21:22] sts.

With RS of work facing, sl centre 40 sts on to a holder, rejoin yarn to next st and K to end.
Next row Cast off 19[21:23] sts, P to end. Work one row. Cast off rem 19[21:22] sts.

FRONT

Work as given for Back to *.
Cont without shaping until Chart row 174 has been completed, so ending with a P row.

Shape neck

Next row K51[55:58] sts, turn and leave rem sts on a spare needle.
Complete left side of neck first. Cast off at beg

Design N.º 23

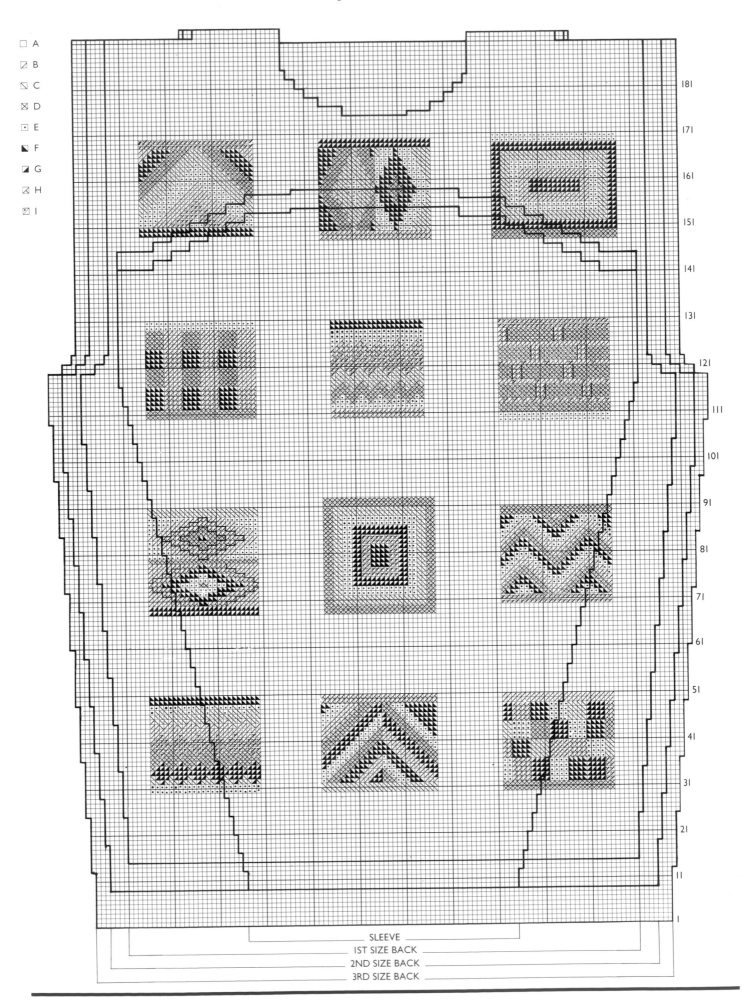

A
B
C
D
E
F
G
H
I

181
171
161
151
141
131
121
111
101
91
81
71
61
51
41
31
21
11
1

SLEEVE
1ST SIZE BACK
2ND SIZE BACK
3RD SIZE BACK

112

'My brother-in-law, Richard, spends a lot of time in Central and Southern America and on his travels he always collects pieces of textiles and ceramics as references for my work. 'Santos' is based on a design he picked up in Guatemala that I have deliberately styled for a man. I enjoy designing for men; their rather formal taste imposes certain restrictions and it is always a challenge to break them slightly, yet still come up with a garment that is popular and very wearable.
As well as proving inspirational to my designing, the very rich bright colourings of 'Santos' were the source of a complete range of cotton yarns that I co-ordinated for Rowan's Summer 1991 collection.'

of next and foll alt rows 5 sts once, 3 sts once, 2 sts twice and one st once. 38[42:45] sts. Cont without shaping until Chart row 190 (row 191 for other side of neck) has been completed, so ending at armhole edge.

Shape shoulder

Cast off 19[21:23] sts at beg of next row. Work one row. Cast off rem 19[21:22] sts. With RS of work facing, sl centre 14 sts on to a holder, rejoin yarn to next st and K to end. Work one row, then complete as given for other side of neck, noting the bracketed exception.

SLEEVES

Using 3¼mm (US3) needles and A, cast on 50 sts. Work 6cm (2½in) in K1, P1 rib, ending with a RS row.
Next row Rib 3, inc in next st, (rib 5, inc in next st) to last 4 sts, rib 4. 58 sts.
Change to 4mm (US6) needles.
Beg with a K row, cont in st st and patt from

Chart, starting at row 9. Inc one st at each end of 5th and every foll 4th row until there are 112 sts. Cont without shaping until Chart row 140[140:144] has been completed, so ending with a P row.

Previous page 'Santos' is a bright and cheerful design comprising rectangles that each contains a different multi-coloured geometric design. Although this was originally designed as a man's sweater it has such universal appeal that Mark had better watch out!

Shape top

Cast off 8 sts at beg of next 2 rows, 4 sts at beg of foll 10 rows and 10 sts at beg of next 2 rows. Cast off rem 36 sts.

NECKBAND

Join right shoulder seam.
Using 3¼mm (US3) needles, A and with RS of work facing, pick up and K19 sts down left front neck, K across 14 sts on holder, pick up and K19 sts up right front neck, one st down right back neck, K across 40 sts on holder and pick up and K one st up left back neck. 94 sts.
Work 6cm (2½in) in K1, P1 rib. Cast off loosely in rib.

TO MAKE UP

Press on WS using a warm iron over a damp cloth. Join left shoulder and neckband seam. Fold neckband in half to inside and slip stitch in position. Set in sleeves. Join side and sleeve seams. Press seams.

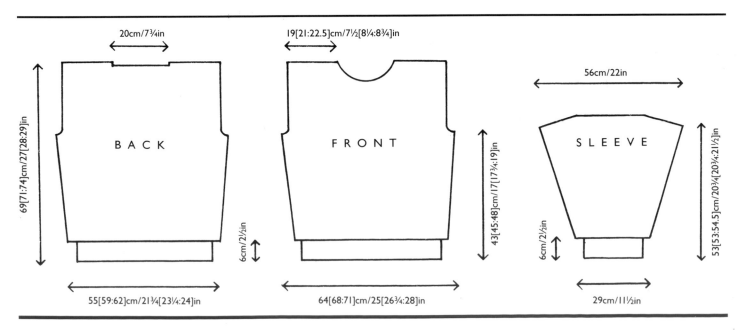

Design N.º 24

Pokoman

A classic cotton sweater is a backdrop for intricate narrow patterned stripes separating broader bands with bold geometric motifs. The ribbed lower edge and cuffs are a clever combination of narrow multi-coloured stripes overlaid with vertical lines of the background colour. 'Pokoman' can also be knitted as a V neck cardigan.

SIZES

To fit chest 107[112:117]cm (42[44:46]in)
Actual size 127[134:140]cm (49½[53:55]in)
Length to shoulder 69.5[72:74.5]cm (27¼[28½:29¼]in)
Sleeve seam 52[52:54.5]cm (20½[20½:21½]in)
Figures in square brackets [] refer to larger sizes; where there is only one set of figures, it applies to all sizes

MATERIALS

7[8:8] × 50g balls of Rowan Handknit DK Cotton in main colour A (Scarlet 255/Black 252)
4[4:5] balls in colour B (Black 252/Scarlet 255)
2[2:2] balls in colour C (Mustard 246)
2[3:3] balls in colour D (True Navy 244/Royal 294)
2[2:2] balls in colour E (Ecru 251)
4[4:5] balls in colour F (Violet 256)
2[2:2] balls in colour G (Peacock 259)
2[3:3] balls in colour H (Clover 266)
1[1:2] × 50g balls of Rowan Fine Chenille in colour I (Cardinal 379)
Pair each of 3¼mm (US3) and 4mm (US6) knitting needles
5 buttons for Cardigan

TENSION

22 sts and 27 rows to 10cm (4in) over patt using 4mm (US6) needles

SWEATER

BACK

Using 3¼mm (US3) needles and B, cast on 107[113:119] sts. Work in multi-colour rib as foll:
1st row (RS) (Using B, P1, K1) to last st, P1.
2nd row Using F, K1, P1, K1, P1, K1, (using A, P1, using F, K1, P1, K1, P1, K1) to end.
3rd row Using F, P1, K1, P1, K1, P1, (using A, K1, using F, P1, K1, P1, K1, P1) to end.
4th-21st rows Rep 2nd and 3rd rows 9 times more, keeping continuity of A, in 2 row stripes as foll: H, E, C, G, H, F, E, G and B.
22nd row Using B, P4[8:3], inc in next st, (P6[5:6], inc in next st) to last 4[8:3] sts, P to end. 122[130:136] sts.
Change to 4mm (US6) needles.

Beg with a K row, cont in st st and patt from Chart, starting at row 15[9:1]. Read odd-numbered (K) rows from right to left and even-numbered (P) rows from left to right. Strand colour not in use loosely across WS of work where appropriate or use small, separate balls of yarn for individual motifs.

'A shop in Brighton sells all manner of artefacts and jewellery from Guatemala. While browsing I discovered a wonderful book on costumes from the area. The woven fabrics intrigued me; many consisted of two-colour patterns that changed every few rows to make a dazzling array of shapes and colour. 'Pokoman' amalgamates the ideas from Guatemalan textiles and pottery, including the use of large geometric motifs set against a deep horizontal stripe.
Although this sweater is in men's sizing, I am all for a woman wearing it. After all, which woman has never borrowed one of her man's sweaters? I know that I am always wearing garments from my menswear collection.'

Work 10 rows. Inc one st at each end of next and every foll 10th row until there are 140[148:154] sts. Cont without shaping until Chart row 110 has been completed, so ending with a P row.

Shape armholes

Cast off 3 sts at beg of next 2 rows, 2 sts at beg of foll 2 rows and one st at beg of next 2 rows. 128[136:142] sts. *
Cont without shaping until Chart row 180 has been completed, so ending with a P row.

Shape shoulders and back neck

Next row Patt 22[24:26] sts, work until there are 22[24:25] sts on right-hand needle, turn. Work one row. Cast off rem 22[24:25] sts. With RS of work facing, sl centre 40 sts on to a holder, rejoin yarn to next st and patt to end.
Next row Cast off 22[24:26] sts, patt to end. Work one row. Cast off rem 22[24:25] sts.

FRONT

Work as given for Back to *.
Cont without shaping until Chart row 164 has been completed, so ending with a P row.

Shape neck

Next row Patt 57[61:64] sts, turn and leave rem sts on a spare needle.
Complete left side of neck first.
Cast off at beg of next and foll alt rows 5 sts once, 3 sts once, 2 sts twice and one st once. 44[48:51] sts. Cont without shaping until Chart row 180 (row 181 for other side of neck) has been completed, so ending at armhole edge.

Shape shoulder

Cast off 22[24:26] sts at beg of next row. Work one row. Cast off rem 22[24:25] sts. With RS of work facing, sl centre 14 sts on to a holder, rejoin yarn to next st and patt to end. Work one row, then complete as given for other side of neck, noting the bracketed exception.

SLEEVES

Using 3¼mm (US3) needles and B, cast on 53 sts. Work 21 rows in multi-colour rib as given for Back welt.
22nd row Using B, P6, inc in next st, (P4, inc in next st) to last 6 sts, P6. 62 sts.
Change to 4mm (US6) needles.
Beg with a K row, cont in st st and patt from

Tijan loved the richly-patterned 'Pokoman' sweater so much that she asked to wear it when everyone went to the country on a horse-riding expedition. These patterns would be familiar to the horsemen of their native South American habitat.

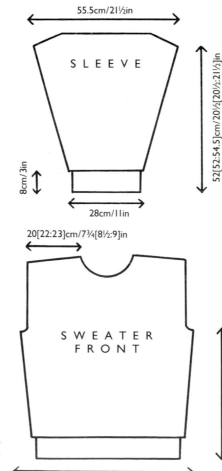

55.5cm/21½in

SLEEVE

52[52:54.5]cm/20½[20½:21½]in

8cm/3in

28cm/11in

20[22:23]cm/7¾[8½:9]in

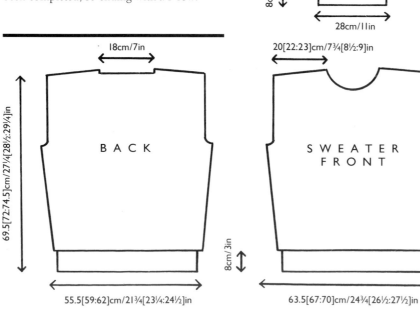

18cm/7in

BACK

69.5[72:74.5]cm/27¼[28½:29¼]in

55.5[59:62]cm/21¾[23¼:24½]in

8cm/3in

SWEATER FRONT

63.5[67:70]cm/24¾[26½:27½]in

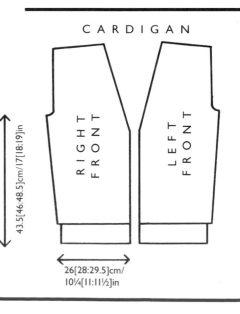

CARDIGAN

RIGHT FRONT

LEFT FRONT

43.5[46:48.5]cm/17[18:19]in

26[28:29.5]cm/10¼[11:11½]in

Design Nº 24

A
B
C
D
E
F
G
H
I

171
161
151
141
131
121
111
101
91
81
71
61
51
41
31
21
11

I

SLEEVE

1ST SIZE RIGHT FRONT — 1ST SIZE LEFT FRONT

1ST SIZE BACK

2ND SIZE RIGHT FRONT — 2ND SIZE LEFT FRONT

2ND SIZE BACK

3RD SIZE RIGHT FRONT — 3RD SIZE LEFT FRONT

3RD SIZE BACK

Design N.º 24

' Textiles from different regions of Guatemala all feature a lot of unusual chalky colours mixed with very positive black and white. These colours together with the very complicated woven patterns started a train of ideas that led to 'Pokoman'. '

Chart, inc one st at each end of 4th and every foll 3rd row until there are 122 sts. Cont without shaping until Chart row 120[120:126] has been completed, so ending with a P row.

Shape top
Cast off 8 sts at beg of next 2 rows, 4 sts at beg of foll 10 rows and 8 sts at beg of next 2 rows. Cast off rem 50 sts.

NECKBAND

Join right shoulder seam. Using 3¼mm (US3) needles, A and with RS of work facing, pick up and K19 sts down left front neck, K across 14 sts on holder, pick up and K19 sts up right front neck, one st down right back neck, K across 40 sts on holder and pick up and K one st up left back neck. 94 sts.
Work 6cm (2½in) in K1, P1 rib. Cast off evenly in rib.

TO MAKE UP

Press on WS of work using a warm iron over a damp cloth. Join left shoulder and neckband seam. Fold neckband in half to inside and slip stitch in position. Set in sleeves. Join side and sleeve seams. Press seams.

CARDIGAN

BACK

Work as given for Back of Sweater.

POCKET LININGS
(make 2)

Using 4mm (US6) needles and A, cast on 28 sts. Beg with a K row, work 38 rows in st st. Cut off yarn. Leave sts on a holder.

LEFT FRONT

Using 3¼mm (US3) needles and B, cast on 53[53:59] sts. Work 21 rows in multi-colour rib as given for Back welt.
22nd row Using B, P6, inc in next st, (rib 9[4:8], inc in next st) to last 6[6:7] sts, P to end. 58[62:65] sts.
Change to 4mm (US6) needles.
Beg with a K row, cont in st st and patt from

'Pokoman', consisting of layer upon layer of bright and subtle colours in ever-changing patterns, is proudly displayed against the horse's gleaming chestnut coat and polished leather saddle.

Chart, starting at row 15[9:1]. Cont in patt, shaping side edge as indicated until Chart row 52[46:38] has been completed.

Place pocket
Next row Patt 6[10:13] sts, sl next 28 sts on to a holder, patt across sts of first pocket lining, patt to end.

Cont in patt from Chart, working shaping at side edge, front edge and armhole as indicated.

RIGHT FRONT

Work as given for Left Front, following the appropriate Chart and placing pocket as foll:
Pocket row Patt 27 sts, sl next 28 sts on to a holder, patt across sts of pocket lining, patt to end.

SLEEVES

Work as given for Sleeves of Sweater.

FRONT BAND

Join shoulder seams.
Using 3¼mm (US3) needles and A, cast on 7 sts.
1st row (RS) K1, (K1, P1) to end.
2nd row K1, (P1, K1) to end.
Rep these 2 rows until band, when slightly stretched, fits up right front edge to shoulder. Sew band in position as you go along. Mark position of buttons with pins – the top one level with start of shaping, the bottom one 1cm (½in) up from lower edge, with the others evenly spaced between.
Cont in rib until band fits all around back neck and down left front, making buttonholes as markers are reached as foll:
Buttonhole row (RS) Rib 3, yo, K2 tog, rib 2. Cont until band reaches cast-on edge of left front, sewing it in position as before. Cast off.

POCKET TOPS

Using 4mm (US6) needles, A and with RS of work facing, K across 28 pocket sts from needle. K one row to mark foldline. Beg with a K row, work 2cm (¾in) in st st. Cast off.

TO MAKE UP

Press on WS of work using a warm iron over a damp cloth. Turn pocket tops to inside at foldline and slip stitch in position. Sew down pocket linings on WS of work. Set in sleeves. Join side and sleeve seams. Press seams. Sew on buttons.

BRIGHT AND
Natural Cree

A truly multi-size garment, 'Cree' fits everyone from a toddler to a giant (or rather, a large man). The classic crew neck sweater with traditional Eskimo Indian symbols, knitted in a mixture of tweed, chenille and double knitting yarns, looks different according to the colourway – natural and earthy here for the adult's version or bright and more colourful for the child's sweater.

SIZES

To fit bust/chest 56-61[66-71:76-81:87-91:96-107:107-117:117-127]cm (22-24[26-28:30-32:34-36:38-42:42-46:46-50]in)
Actual size 74[82:99:106:148:154:158]cm (29[33:39:41½:58:60½:62]in)
Length to shoulder 37[40:45:50:67:69:71]cm (14½[15¾:17¾:19½:26½:27:27¾]in)
Sleeve seam 21[26:30:36:49:49:50]cm (8¼[10¼:11¾:14:19¼:19¼:19½]in)
Figures in square brackets [] refer to larger sizes; where there is only one set of figures, it applies to all sizes

MATERIALS

Child's Sweater (first 4 sizes only)
4[4:5:5] × 50g balls of Rowan Fox Tweed in main colour A (Black 854)
1 × 50g ball of Rowan Fine Chenille in each of four colours, B (Purple 384), C (Seville 387), D (Turquoise 383) and E (Cardinal 379)
1 × 50g ball of Rowan Designer DK in each of two colours, F (tan 627) and G (stone 656)

Adult's Sweater (last 3 sizes only)
12[12:13] × 50g balls of Fox Tweed in main colour A (Seal 852)
2 × 50g balls of Rowan Fine Chenille in colour B (Black 377)
2 × 50g balls of Rowan Designer DK in each of two colours, C (black 62) and D (ecru 649)
Pair each of 3¼mm (US3) and 4mm (US6) knitting needles

TENSION

21 sts and 27 rows to 10cm (4in) over patt using 4mm (US6) needles

BACK

Using 3¼mm (US3) needles and A, cast on 70[76:92:98:104:108:112] sts. Work 4[4:5:6:8:8:8]cm (1½[1½:2:2½:3:3:3]in) in K1, P1 rib, ending with a RS row.
Next row Rib 7[5:7:3:5:4:6], inc in next st, (rib 7[5:6:6:2:2:2], inc in next st) to last 6[4:7:3:5:4:6] sts, rib to end. 78[88:104:112:136:142:146] sts.
Change to 4mm (US6) needles.
Beg with a K row, work 0[0:0:0:4:4:4] rows in st st. Commence patt, working from appropriate Chart, reading odd-numbered (K) rows from right to left and even-numbered (P) rows from left to right and using small, separate balls of yarn for individual motifs.

Last 3 sizes only
Cont in patt, inc one st at each end of 5th and every foll 6th row until there are 156[162:166] sts, working extra sts into patt.

All sizes
Cont in patt until work measures 23[24:28:32:42:44:46]cm (9[9½:11:12½:16½:17¼:18]in) from beg, ending with a P row.

Left *William, wearing his colourful 'Cree' sweater, thinks that he might have discovered the dragon's lair.*
Overleaf *Brigit, in a natural 'Cree' sweater, accompanies William's cousin Thomas on his search for the monsters.*

Design N° 25

□ A
⊠ B
◪ C
⊟ D
⊘ E
⧄ F
⊡ G

1ST SIZE SLEEVE
2ND SIZE SLEEVE
3RD SIZE SLEEVE
4TH SIZE SLEEVE

1ST SIZE BACK
2ND SIZE BACK
3RD SIZE BACK
4TH SIZE BACK

CHART FOR MAN'S SWEATER

□ A
⊠ B
⊡ C
⊠ D

REPEAT 32 STS
5TH, 6TH AND 7TH SIZES SLEEVES
5TH SIZE BACK
6TH SIZE BACK
7TH SIZE BACK

123

Design N° 25

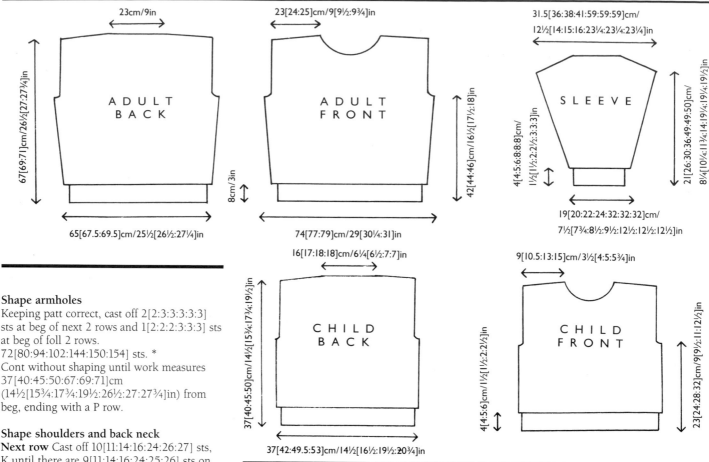

Shape armholes
23cm/9in
ADULT BACK
67[69:71]cm/26½[27:27¾]in
65[67.5:69.5]cm/25½[26½:27¼]in

23[24:25]cm/9[9½:9¾]in
ADULT FRONT
8cm/3in
42[44:46]cm/16½[17½:18]in
74[77:79]cm/29[30¼:31]in

31.5[36:38:41:59:59:59]cm/12½[14:15:16:23¼:23¼:23¼]in
SLEEVE
4[4:5:6:8:8:8]cm/1½[1½:2:2½:3:3:3]in
21[26:30:36:49:49:50]cm/8¼[10¼:11¾:14:19¼:19¼:19½]in
19[20:22:24:32:32:32]cm/7½[7¾:8½:9½:12½:12½:12½]in

16[17:18:18]cm/6¼[6½:7:7]in
CHILD BACK
37[40:45:50]cm/14½[15¾:17¾:19½]in
37[42:49.5:53]cm/14½[16½:19½:20¾]in

9[10.5:13:15]cm/3½[4:5:5¾]in
CHILD FRONT
4[4:5:6]cm/1½[1½:2:2½]in
23[24:28:32]cm/9[9½:11:12½]in

Shape armholes

Keeping patt correct, cast off 2[2:3:3:3:3:3] sts at beg of next 2 rows and 1[2:2:2:3:3:3] sts at beg of foll 2 rows.
72[80:94:102:144:150:154] sts. *
Cont without shaping until work measures 37[40:45:50:67:69:71]cm (14½[15¾:17¾:19½:26½:27:27¾]in) from beg, ending with a P row.

Shape shoulders and back neck

Next row Cast off 10[11:14:16:24:26:27] sts, K until there are 9[11:14:16:24:25:26] sts on right-hand needle, turn and complete right side of neck first.
Patt one row. Cast off rem 9[11:14:16:24:25:26] sts.
With RS of work facing, sl centre 34[36:38:38:48:48:48] sts on to a holder, rejoin yarn to next st and patt to end.
Next row Cast off 10[11:14:16:24:26:27] sts, patt to end.
Patt one row. Cast off rem 9[11:14:16:24:25:26] sts.

FRONT

Work as given for Back to *.
Cont without shaping until work measures 32[35:39:44:61:63:65]cm (12½[13¾:15¼:17¼:24:24¾:25½]in) from beg, ending with a P row.

Shape neck

Next row Patt 31[35:41:45:63:66:68] sts, turn and leave rem sts on a spare needle.
Complete left side of neck first.
Cast off at beg of next and foll alt rows 5[5:5:5:4:4:4] sts once,
4[4:3:3:4:4:4] sts once, 2[2:2:2:4:4:4] sts once, 1[2:2:2:1:1:1] sts once, 0[0:1:1:1:1:1] st once and 0[0:0:0:1:1:1] sts once.
19[22:28:32:48:51:53] sts. Cont without shaping until front matches back to shoulder, ending at armhole edge.

Shape shoulder

Cast off 10[11:14:16:24:26:27] sts at beg of next row. Work one row. Cast off rem

9[11:14:16:24:25:26] sts.
With RS of work facing, sl centre 10[10:12:12:18:18:18] sts on to a holder, rejoin yarn to next st and patt to end.
Next row Work to end.
Complete as given for other side of neck and shoulder.

SLEEVES

Using 3¼mm (US3) needles and A, cast on 36[36:40:44:48:48:48] sts. Work 4[4:5:6:8:8:8]cm (1½[1½:2:2½:3:3:3]in) in K1, P1 rib, ending with a RS row.
Next row Rib 4[3:5:4:5:5:5], inc in next st, (rib 8[5:5:6:1:1:1], inc in next st) to last 4[2:4:4:4:4:4] sts, rib to end.
40[42:46:50:68:68:68] sts.
Change to 4mm (US6) needles.
Beg with a K row, work 4 rows st st. Cont in st st and patt from Chart, inc one st at each end of first and every foll 3rd row until there are 66[76:80:86:124:124:124] sts, working extra sts into patt.
Cont without shaping until sleeve measures 21[26:30:36:49:49:50]cm (8¼[10¼:11¾:14:19¼:19¼:19½]in) from beg, ending with a P row.

Shape top

Cast off 7[8:7:8:6:6:6] sts at beg of next 2 rows, 4 sts at beg of foll 6[6:8:8:10:10:10] rows and 6[8:8:8:10:10:10] sts at beg of next 2 rows. Cast off rem 16[20:18:22:52:52:52] sts.

NECKBAND

Join right shoulder seam.
Using 3¼mm (US3) needles, A and with RS of work facing, pick up and K19[20:22:22:23:23:23] sts down left front neck, K across 10[10:12:12:18:18:18] front neck sts on holder, pick up and K19[20:22:22:23:23:23] sts up right front neck, one st from right back neck, K across 34[36:38:38:48:48:48] back neck sts on holder and pick up and K one st from left back neck. 84[88:96:96:114:114:114] sts.
Work 6cm (2½in) in K1, P1 rib. Cast off loosely in rib.

TO MAKE UP

Press on WS using a warm iron over a damp cloth. Join left shoulder and neckband seam. Fold neckband in half to inside and slip stitch in position. Set in sleeves. Join side and sleeve seams. Press seams.

'In 1989 the Museum Of Mankind in London had a marvellous exhibition on the Eskimo Indian tribes of Northern Canada including the Cree. I have used some of the symbols from their woven baskets in this design.'

Design Nº 26

Tile

*Combining cotton yarns and chenille for richness of colour and stitch
definition, 'Tile' is a crew neck sweater in men's sizing with intricate intarsia
patterning inspired by Victorian ceramics.*

SIZES

To fit chest 96-102[107-112:117-122:122-
127]cm (38-40[42-44:46-48:48-50]in)
Actual size 115[125:134:141]cm
(45¼[49¼:52¾:55½]in)
Length to shoulder 69[71:74:76]cm
(27[28:29:30]in)
Sleeve seam 53[53:53:54.5]cm
(20¾[20¾:20¾:21½]in)
Figures in square brackets [] refer to larger
sizes; where there is only one set of figures, it
applies to all sizes

MATERIALS

Colourway A
11[12:12:13] × 50g balls of Rowan DK Cotton
in main colour A (True Navy 244)
2[2:3:3] × 50g balls of Rowan Fine Chenille
in colour B (Lacquer 388)
4[4:5:5] × 50g balls of DK Cotton in colour
C (Sky 264)
2[2:2:3] balls of Fine Chenille in colour D
(Turquoise 383)
3[3:4:4] balls of Fine Chenille in colour E
(Mole 380)
1[1:1:2] balls of DK Cotton in colour F (Linen
299)
3[3:4:4] balls of DK Cotton in colour G
(Snow Thistle 288)

Colourway B
Colour A is DK Cotton in Ecru 251
Colour B is Fine Chenille in Mole 380
Colour C is Fine Chenille in Box 393
Colour D is Sea Breeze in Turkish Plum 529 –
use double throughout
Colour E is Fine Chenille in Lacquer 388
Colour F is DK Cotton in Bathstone 257
Colour G is DK Cotton in True Navy 244
Pair each of 3¼mm (US3) and 4mm (US6)
knitting needles
5[5:6:6] buttons for Cardigan

TENSION

23 sts and 27 rows to 10cm (4in) over patt
using 4mm (US6) needles

SWEATER

BACK

Using 3¼mm (US3) needles and A, cast on
96[100:104:110] sts.
1st row (RS) (K1 tbl, P1) to end.
Rep this row to form twisted rib for 8cm
(3in), ending with a RS row.
Next row Rib 9[12:8:8], inc in next st, (rib
3[2:2:2], inc in next st) to last 10[12:8:8] sts,
rib to end. 116[126:134:142] sts.
Change to 4mm (US6) needles.
Beg with a K row, cont in st st and patt from
Chart, starting at row 21[15:7:1] and reading
odd-numbered (K) rows from right to left and
even-numbered (P) rows from left to right.
Strand colour not in use loosely across WS of
work where appropriate or use small, separate
balls of yarn for individual motifs.
Work 10 rows, then inc one st at each end of
next and every foll 10th row until there are
132[144:154:162] sts. Cont without shaping
until Chart row 114 has been completed, so
ending with a P row.

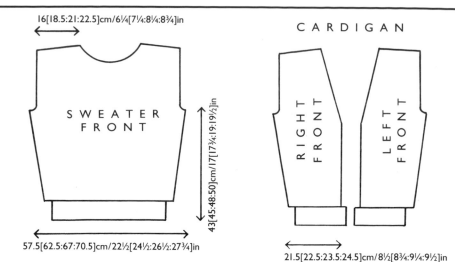

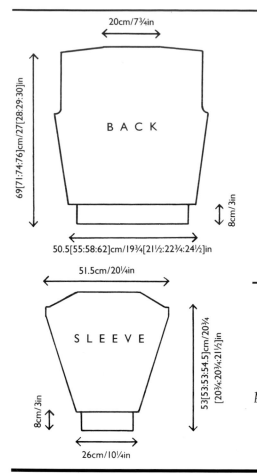

20cm/7¾in

BACK

69[71:74:76]cm/27[28:29:30]in

8cm/3in

50.5[55:58:62]cm/19¾[21½:22¾:24½]in

16[18.5:21:22.5]cm/6¼[7¼:8¼:8¾]in

SWEATER FRONT

43[45:48:50]cm/17[17¾:19:19½]in

CARDIGAN

RIGHT FRONT

LEFT FRONT

57.5[62.5:67:70.5]cm/22½[24½:26½:27¾]in

21.5[22.5:23.5:24.5]cm/8½[8¾:9¼:9½]in

51.5cm/20¼in

SLEEVE

53[53:53:54.5]cm/20¾[20¾:20¾:21½]in

8cm/3in

26cm/10¼in

'To create areas of pattern within a pattern in a strict outline is always a challenge. William de Morgan used many shades of blue and green in his work. I wanted to reproduce the richness of these colours not only in the patterning, but in the yarn as well. To achieve this effect I have used a lot of chenille yarn for its textured depth and density of colour.'

Shape armholes

Cast off 3 sts at beg of next 2 rows, 2 sts at beg of foll 2 rows and one st at beg of next 2 rows. 120[132:142:150] sts. * Cont without shaping until Chart row 184 has been completed, so ending with a P row.

Shape shoulders and back neck

Next row Cast off 18[21:26:27] sts, K until there are 19[22:22:25] sts on right-hand needle, turn and complete right side of neck first.
Work one row. Cast off rem sts.
With RS of work facing, sl centre 46 sts on to a holder, rejoin yarn to next st and patt to end.
Next row Cast off 18[21:26:27] sts, patt to end.
Work one row. Cast off rem sts.

FRONT

Work as given for Back to *. Cont without shaping until Chart row 168 has been completed, so ending with a P row.

Shape neck

Next row Patt 53[59:64:68] sts, turn and leave rem sts on a spare needle.
Complete left side of neck first. ** Cast off at beg of next and foll alt rows 6 sts once, 4 sts once, 3 sts once, 2 sts once and one st once. 37[43:48:52] sts. Cont without shaping until Chart row 184 (row 185 for other side of neck) has been completed, so ending at armhole edge.

Shape shoulder

Cast off 18[21:26:27] sts at beg of next row.
Work one row. Cast off rem 19[22:22:25] sts.
With RS of work facing, sl centre 14 sts on to a holder, rejoin yarn to next st and patt to end. Work one row. Complete as given for other side of neck from ** to end, noting the bracketed exception.

SLEEVES

Using 3¼mm (US3) needles and A, cast on 48 sts. Work 8cm (3in) in twisted rib as given for Back welt, ending with a RS row.
Next row Rib 2, inc in next st, (rib 3, inc in next st) to last st, rib 1. 60 sts.
Change to 4mm (US6) needles.
Beg with a K row, cont in st st and patt from Chart, starting at row 15. Inc one st at each end of 4th and every foll 3rd row until there are 118 sts. Cont without shaping until Chart row 136[136:136:140] has been completed, so ending with a P row.

Shape top

Cast off 5 sts at beg of next 2 rows, 4 sts at beg of foll 10 rows and 14 sts at beg of next 2 rows. Cast off rem 40 sts.

NECKBAND

Join right shoulder seam.
Using 3¼mm (US3) needles, A and with RS of work facing, pick up and K24 sts down left front neck, K across 14 sts on holder, pick up and K24 sts up right front neck, one st down right back neck, K across 46 back neck sts on

holder and pick up and K one st up left back neck. 110 sts.
Work 6cm (2½in) in twisted rib. Cast off evenly in rib.

TO MAKE UP

Press on WS using a warm iron over a damp cloth. Join left shoulder and neckband seam. Fold neckband in half to inside and slip stitch in position. Set in sleeves. Join side and sleeve seams. Press seams.

CARDIGAN

BACK

Work as given for Back of Sweater.

LEFT FRONT

Using 3¼mm (US3) needles and A, cast on 50[52:54:56] sts.
1st row (RS) (K1 tbl, P1) to last 2 sts, K1 tbl, K1.

Inspired by the complex designs used in Victorian ceramics, 'Tile' is worn here by Mark who is relaxing in more natural surroundings. There are also instructions for a cardigan version of this design.

Design № 26

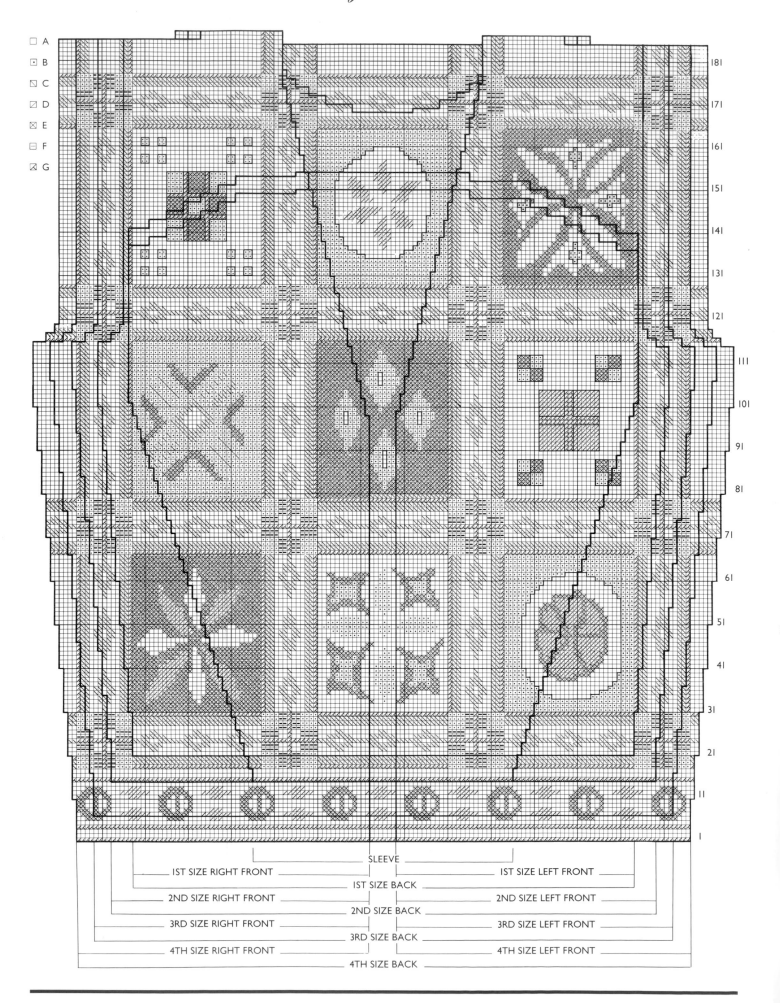

A
B
C
D
E
F
G

181
171
161
151
141
131
121
111
101
91
81
71
61
51
41
31
21
11
1

SLEEVE
1ST SIZE RIGHT FRONT   1ST SIZE LEFT FRONT
1ST SIZE BACK
2ND SIZE RIGHT FRONT   2ND SIZE LEFT FRONT
2ND SIZE BACK
3RD SIZE RIGHT FRONT   3RD SIZE LEFT FRONT
3RD SIZE BACK
4TH SIZE RIGHT FRONT   4TH SIZE LEFT FRONT
4TH SIZE BACK

'*The work of William de Morgan, who designed ceramics around the turn of the century, is full to the brim with minute, complicated patterns. I really admire the intricacy of the shapes and how they work together as a design. With 'Tile' I wanted to balance designing with more fluid (often floral) motifs and rich, deep colours.*'

2nd row K1, (P1, K1 tbl) to last st, P1.
Rep these 2 rows once more.
Next row (Buttonhole row) Rib to last 5 sts, yfwd, K2 tog, rib 3.
Work 15 rows in rib, then rep buttonhole row again. Cont in rib until work measures 8cm (3in) from beg, ending with a RS row.
Next row Rib 6 and place these sts on a safety-pin for buttonhole band, rib 2[3:1:8], inc in next st, (rib 3[2:2:1], inc in next st) to last 1[3:1:7] sts, rib to end. 55[60:64:68] sts.
* Change to 4mm (US6) needles.
Beg with a K row, cont in st st and patt from Chart, starting at row 21[15:7:1]. Work 10 rows, then inc one st at beg (for Right Front, read 'end' here) of next and every foll 10th row until there are 62[68:73:77] sts. Cont without shaping until Chart row 99 (row 98 for Right Front) has been completed, so ending at front edge.

Shape front edge
Cont to inc at side edge as before once more, *at the same time* dec one st at front edge at beg of next and every foll 4th row until Chart row 114 (row 115 for Right Front) has been completed.

Shape armhole
Cont to dec at front edge on every 4th row, *at the same time* cast off 3 sts at beg of next row, 2 sts at beg of foll alt row and one st at beg of next alt row. 52[58:63:67] sts. (51[57:62:66] sts for Right Front)
Keeping armhole edge straight, cont to dec at front edge as before until 37[43:48:52] sts rem. Cont without shaping until Chart row 184 (row 185 for Right Front) has been completed, so ending at armhole edge.

Shape shoulder
Cast off 18[21:26:27] sts at beg of next row.
Work one row. Cast off rem 19[22:22:25] sts.

RIGHT FRONT

Using 3¼mm (US3) needles and A, cast on 50[52:54:56] sts.

The clear sky and rich azure of the Mediterranean make a perfect backdrop for this sweater with its concentration on the colour blue. Navy, sky blue and turquoise intermingle with red and brown to create an intensity of colour – an effect that is heightened by combining smooth cotton yarn with velvety chenille.

1st row (RS) K1, (P1, K1 tbl) to last st, P1.
2nd row (K1 tbl, P1) to last 2 sts, K1 tbl, K1.
Rep these 2 rows until work measures 8cm (3in) from beg, ending with a RS row.
Next row Rib 2[3:1:8], inc in next st, (rib 3[2:2:1], inc in next st) to last 7[9:7:13] sts, rib 1[3:1:7], turn and place last 6 sts on a safety-pin for button band. 55[60:64:68] sts.
Complete as given for Left Front from * to end, noting the bracketed exceptions.

SLEEVES

Work as given for Sweater Sleeves.

BUTTON BAND

Join shoulder seams.
Using 3¼mm (US3) needles, A and with WS of work facing, sl 6 sts from Right Front safety-pin on to left-hand needle, inc in first st, then rib to end. Cont in rib until band, when slightly stretched, fits up Right Front edge and round to centre back neck. Cast off.
Sew band in position.
Mark position of buttons with pins. The last is level with start of front shaping, with 2[2:3:3] more evenly spaced between that and buttonhole at top of welt.

BUTTONHOLE BAND

Using 3¼mm (US3) needles, A and with RS of work facing, sl 6 sts from Left Front safety-pin on to left-hand needle, inc in first st, rib to end. Cont in rib until band fits round to centre back neck, making buttonholes on a RS row as markers are reached as foll:

Buttonhole row Rib 2, yfwd, K2 tog, rib 3.
Sew band in position, joining seam at centre back neck.

TO MAKE UP

Press on WS using a warm iron over a damp cloth. Set in sleeves. Join side and sleeve seams. Press seams. Sew on buttons.

Design N° 27

Bear

Although it has been designed in men's sizing, this crew neck sweater looks equally good on a woman. Broad horizontal bands of Fair Isle patterns and intarsia motifs in chenille stand out against a dark tweed background.

SIZES

To fit chest 102[107:112]cm 40[42:44]in
Actual size 121[124:128]cm (47½[49:50]in)
Length to shoulder 62[63:63]cm
(24½[24¾:24¾]in)
Sleeve seam 52[52:53.5]cm (20½[20½:21]in)
Figures in square brackets [] refer to larger sizes; where there is only one set of figures, it applies to all sizes

MATERIALS

9[9:10] × 50g hanks of Rowan Fox Tweed DK in main colour A (Black 854 – colourway 1 or Wren 850 – colourway 2)
3[3:4] balls in colour B (Wren 850 – col 1 or Black 854 – col 2)
2[2:2] × 50g balls of Rowan Fine Chenille in colour C (Lacquer 388 – col 1 or Turquoise 383 – col 2)
2[2:2] balls in colour D (Turquoise 383 – col 1 or Lacquer 388 – col 2)
Pair each of 3¼mm (US3) and 4mm (US6) knitting needles

TENSION

23½ sts and 29 rows to 10cm (4in) over intarsia patt using 4mm (US6) needles

BACK

Using 3¼mm (US3) needles and A, cast on 120[122:126] sts. Work 6cm (2½in) in K1, P1 rib, ending with a RS row.
Next row Rib 7[3:5], inc in next st, (rib 4, inc in next st) to last 7[3:5] sts, rib to end. 142[146:150] sts.
Change to 4mm (US6) needles.

With her sweater borrowed from the men, Monica sets out on the range for a day with the horses. 'Bear' is a stylish design that complements casual clothes especially denim jeans.

Beg with a K row, cont in st st and patt from Chart, starting at row 5[1:1]. Read odd-numbered (K) rows from right to left and even-numbered (P) rows from left to right. Strand colours not in use loosely across WS of work where appropriate or use a small, separate ball of yarn for individual motifs. Cont in patt until Chart row 94 has been completed, so ending with a P row.

Shape armholes
Cast off 3 sts at beg of next 4 rows.
130[134:138] sts. *
Cont without shaping until Chart row 166 has been completed, so ending with a P row.

Shape shoulders and back neck
Next row Cast off 19[21:23] sts, K until there are 24 sts on right-hand needle, turn.
Work one row. Cast off rem 24 sts.
With RS of work facing, sl centre 44 sts on to a holder, rejoin yarn to next st and K to end.
Next row Cast off 19[21:23] sts, P to end.
Work one row. Cast off rem 24 sts.

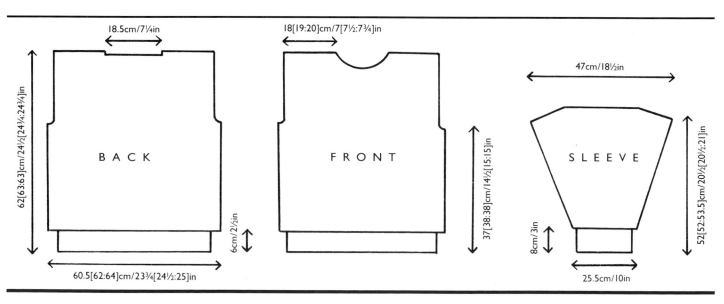

Design № 27

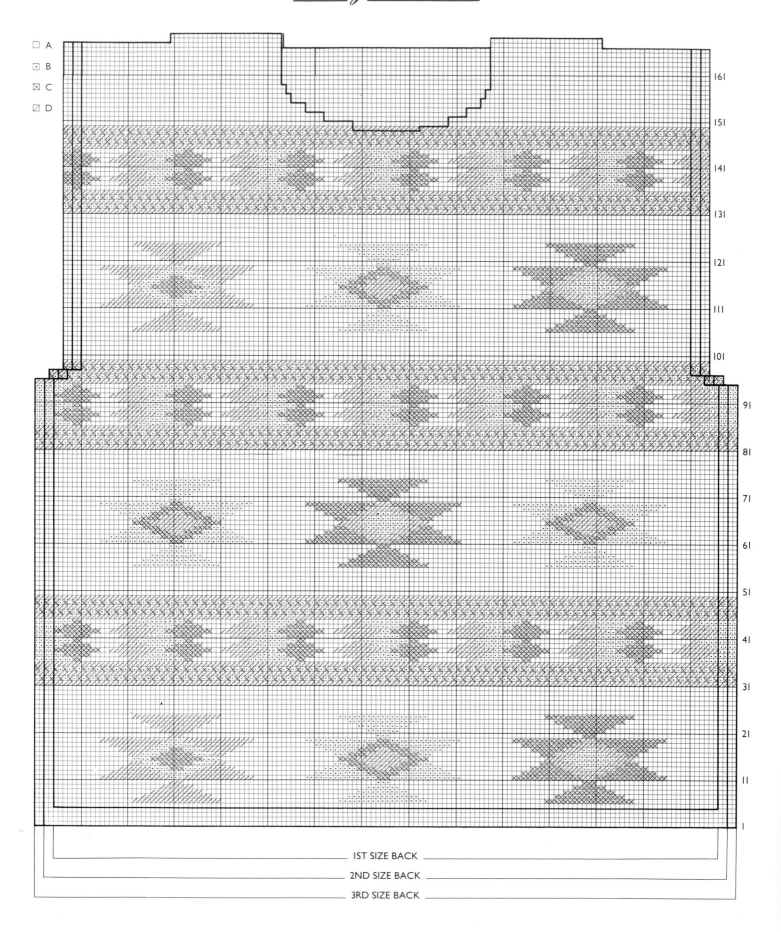

A
B
C
D

161
151
141
131
121
111
101
91
81
71
61
51
41
31
21
11
1

1ST SIZE BACK
2ND SIZE BACK
3RD SIZE BACK

Design Nº 27

'I have always been fascinated by the designs of the American Indians: the balance in their patterns is visually very pleasing. One of the tribes that fascinates me is the Inuit. Although many of them are integrated into the white community, they still retain their traditional crafts such as weaving and painting. The symbols used in 'Bear' originate from a totem pole.'

SLEEVE

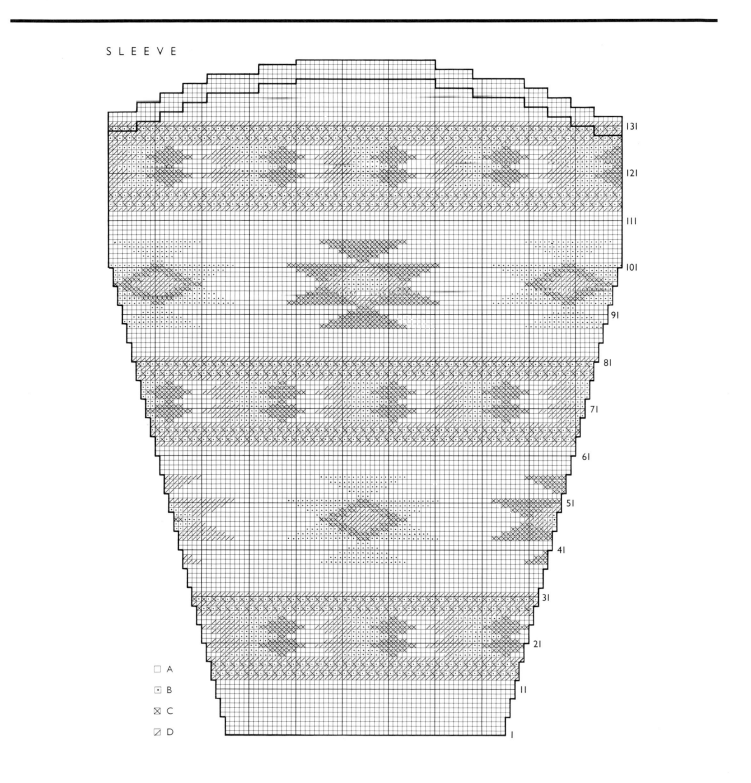

□ A
· B
⊠ C
⊘ D

foll 4th row until there are 110 sts. Cont without shaping until Chart row 128[128:132] has been completed, so ending with a P row.

Shape top
Cast off 6 sts at beg of next 2 rows, 5 sts at beg of foll 6 rows, 11 sts at beg of next 2 rows and 8 sts at beg of foll 2 rows. Cast off rem 30 sts.

NECKBAND
Join right shoulder seam.
Using 3¼mm (US3) needles, A and with RS of work facing, pick up and K27 sts down left front neck, K across 14 sts on holder, pick up and K27 sts up right front neck, one st down right back neck, K across 44 sts on holder and pick up and K one st up left back neck. 114 sts.
Work 6cm (2½in) in K1, P1 rib. Cast off loosely in rib.

TO MAKE UP
Press on WS using a warm iron over a damp cloth. Join left shoulder and neckband seams. Fold neckband in half to inside and slip stitch in position. Set in sleeves. Join side and sleeve seams. Press seams.

FRONT
Work as given for Back to *
Cont without shaping until Chart row 148 has been completed, so ending with a P row.

Shape neck
Next row Patt 58[60:62] sts, turn and leave rem sts on a spare needle.
Complete left side of neck first. Cast off at beg of next and foll alt rows 6 sts once, 4 sts once, 3 sts once and one st twice. 43[45:47] sts. Cont without shaping until Chart row 166 (row 167 for other side of neck) has been completed, ending at armhole edge.

Shape shoulder
Cast off 19[21:23] sts at beg of next row.
Work one row. Cast off rem 24 sts.
With RS of work facing, sl centre 14 sts on to a holder, rejoin yarn to next st and patt to end. Work one row, then complete as given for other side of neck, noting the bracketed exception.

SLEEVES
Using 3¼mm (US3) needles and A, cast on 48 sts. Work 8cm (3in) in K1, P1 rib, ending with a RS row.
Next row Rib 2, inc in next st, (rib 3, inc in next st) to last st, rib 1. 60 sts.
Change to 4mm (US6) needles.
Beg with a K row, cont in st st and patt from Chart, inc one st at each end of 5th and every

'Bear', with its distinctive Indian-style patterns, blends into the rocky terrain of its natural habitat.

Saddle BLANKET

Contrasting forces of subtle and bold vertical stripes, knitted in stocking stitch and a mixture of tweed and double knitting yarns, make an interesting fabric for this loose, boxy jacket. The V neckline features an inset patterned collar trimmed at the lower edges with beaded tassels.

SIZES

To fit bust 81-87[91-96:102-107]cm (32-34[36-38:40-42]in)
Actual size 112.5[122:132.5]cm (44½[48:52]in)
Length to shoulder 60.5[63.5:66.5]cm (23¾[25:26¼]in)
Sleeve seam 49.5cm (19½in)
Figures in square brackets [] refer to larger sizes; where there is only one set of figures, it applies to all sizes

MATERIALS

10[10:11] × 50g hanks of Rowan Fox Tweed in main colour A (Seal 852)
1[1:2] hanks in colour B (Wren 850)
2[3:3] × 50g balls of Rowan Designer DK in colour C (Black 62)
1[1:1] ball in colour D (ruby 673)
3[3:4] balls in colour E (sky blue 665)
1[1:1] ball in colour F (honey 675)
1[1:1] ball in colour G (chestnut 662)
1[1:1] ball in colour H (pale green 664)
Pair each of 3¼mm (US3), 3¾mm (US5) and 4mm (US6) knitting needles
6[6:7] buttons
Beads for tassels if required

TENSION

24 sts and 27 rows to 10cm (4in) over vertical stripe patt using 4mm (US6) needles

BACK

Using 3¼mm (US3) needles and A, cast on 120[132:146] sts.
1st row (RS) (K1, P1) to end.
2nd row (P1, K1) to end.
Rep these 2 rows to form moss st for 2cm (¾in), ending with a WS row.
Change to 4mm (US6) needles.
Beg with a K row, cont in st st and work 10 rows in stripe patt from Chart 1, reading odd-numbered (K) rows from right to left and even-numbered (P) rows from left to right.

Strand colour not in use loosely across WS of work where appropriate or use small, separate balls of yarn for individual sets of stripes. Cont in stripes as set, inc one st at each end of next and every foll 10th row until there are 134[146:158] sts. Cont without shaping until work measures 33[36:39]cm (13[14:15¼]in) from beg, ending with a P row.

Shape armholes

Cast off 3 sts at beg of next 2 rows, 2 sts at beg of foll 2 rows and one st at beg of next 2 rows. 122[134:146] sts. Cont without shaping until work measures 57.5[60.5:63.5]cm (22½[23¾:25]in) from beg, ending with a P row.

Shape back neck

Next row Patt 46[52:58] sts, turn and leave rem sts on a spare needle.
Complete right side of neck first.
Cast off 9 sts at beg of next row and 4 sts at beg of foll alt row. 33[39:45] sts. Work 4

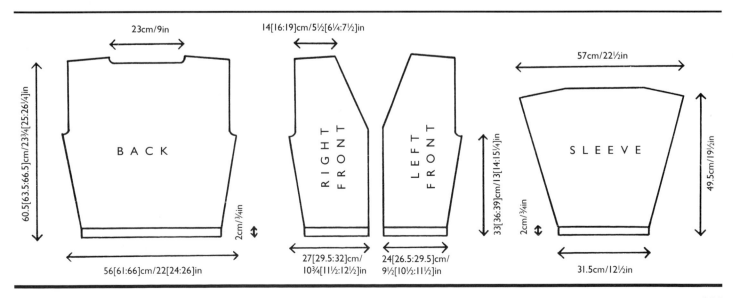

23cm/9in

14[16:19]cm/5½[6¼:7½]in

57cm/22½in

BACK

60.5[63.5:66.5]cm/23¾[25:26¼]in

2cm/¾in

56[61:66]cm/22[24:26]in

RIGHT FRONT

LEFT FRONT

27[29.5:32]cm/ 10¾[11½:12½]in

24[26.5:29.5]cm/ 9½[10½:11½]in

33[36:39]cm/13[14:15¼]in

SLEEVE

2cm/¾in

31.5cm/12½in

49.5cm/19½in

■ Work in moss st in C
□ A
☒ B
☑ C
☒ D
☑ E
☒ F
☐ G
◪ H

CHART 2

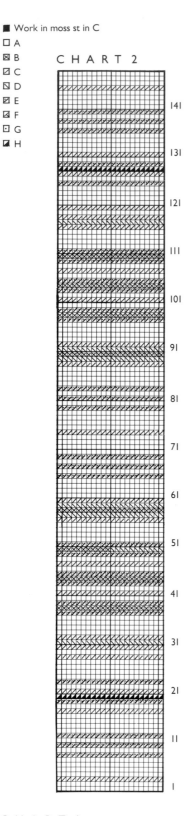

141
131
121
111
101
91
81
71
61
51
41
31
21
11
1

rows without shaping, so ending at armhole edge.

Shape shoulder
Cast off 17[20:23] sts at beg of next row. Work one row. Cast off rem 16[19:22] sts. With RS of work facing, rejoin yarn to next st and cast off centre 30 sts, patt to end. Work one row, then complete as given for other side of neck.

LEFT FRONT

Using 3¼mm (US3) needles and A, cast on 58[64:71] sts. Work 2cm (¾in) in moss st, ending with a WS row.
Change to 4mm (US6) needles.
Beg with a K row, cont in st st and work 10 rows in stripe patt from Chart 1. Cont in stripes, inc one st at beg (for Right Front, read 'end' here) of next and every foll 10th row until there are 65[71:77] sts.
Cont without shaping until Front measures same as Back to underarm, ending with a P row (for Right Front, end with a K row here).

Shape armhole
Cast off 3 sts at beg of next row, 2 sts at beg of foll alt row and one st at beg of next alt row. 59[65:71] sts. Work 2 rows without shaping, so ending at front edge.

Shape front edge
Cast off 2 sts at beg of next and 7 foll alt rows, then dec one st at beg of every foll alt row until 33[39:45] sts rem. Cont without shaping until Front measures same as Back to shoulder, ending at armhole edge.

Shape shoulder
Cast off 17[20:23] sts at beg of next row. Work one row. Cast off rem 16[19:22] sts.

RIGHT FRONT

Work as given for Left Front, following the appropriate section of Chart 1 and noting the bracketed exceptions.

SLEEVES

Using 3¼mm (US3) needles and A, cast on 66 sts. Work 2cm (¾in) in moss st, ending with a WS row.
Change to 4mm (US6) needles.
Beg with a K row, cont in st st and horizontal stripes as shown in Chart 2, inc one st at each end of 4th and every foll 5th row until there are 120 sts. Work 4 rows without shaping, so ending with a P row.

CHART 3

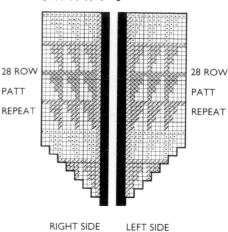

28 ROW PATT REPEAT   28 ROW PATT REPEAT

RIGHT SIDE   LEFT SIDE

Pam displays her talents as a horsewoman wearing a jacket that is inspired by the fabric woven and worn by Afghan tribesmen.

Shape top
Cast off 5 sts at beg of next 2 rows, 4 sts at beg of foll 6 rows and 15 sts at beg of next 2 rows. Cast off rem 56 sts.

COLLAR

LEFT SIDE

Join both shoulder seams.
Using 3¾mm (US5) needles and C, cast on 2 sts.
Next row K1, P1.
Next row P1, K1.
Beg with a K row start at 3rd row of Chart, cont in st st and patt from Chart 3, keeping 2

CHART 1

10
8
6
4
2

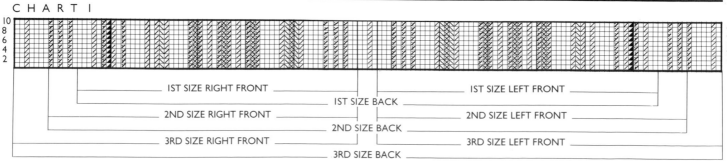

9
7
5
3
1

IST SIZE RIGHT FRONT —————— IST SIZE LEFT FRONT
IST SIZE BACK
2ND SIZE RIGHT FRONT —————— 2ND SIZE LEFT FRONT
2ND SIZE BACK
3RD SIZE RIGHT FRONT —————— 3RD SIZE LEFT FRONT
3RD SIZE BACK

sts in moss st as set throughout *at the same time* cast on 2 sts at beg of next and every foll alt row until there are 16 sts. Cont without shaping, rep 28 patt rows as indicated, until shorter straight edge of collar fits all round neck edge from end of left front shaping up to shoulder and across back neck to right shoulder. Cast off.

RIGHT SIDE

Work as given for left side, reversing shaping and working until straight edge fits up right front from end of shaping to shoulder.

BUTTON BAND

Using 3¼mm (US3) needles and A, cast on 5 sts. Work in moss st until band, when slightly stretched, fits up right front edge to start of shaping. Cast off.
Mark position of buttons on band, the first to come 1cm (½in) above cast-on edge, the last 1cm (½in) below cast-off edge with the others evenly spaced between.

BUTTONHOLE BAND

Work as given for Button Band, making buttonholes as markers are reached as foll:
1st buttonhole row Patt one st, cast off next 2 sts, patt to end.
2nd buttonhole row Patt to end, casting on 2 sts over those cast off in previous row.

TO MAKE UP

Press on WS of work using a warm iron over a damp cloth. Join ends of collar and sew in position, matching shaping and with seam at right shoulder. Sew front bands in position. Set in sleeves. Join side and sleeve seams. Press seams. Sew on buttons. Make beaded tassels in A and sew to lower edge of collar if required.

'*Amongst the Afghan tribes it is traditional to weave cloth for many purposes – tents, horse blankets and clothing. Although their habitat is particularly barren, the weavings are stylish with sophisticated colourings of stripes and geometric florals. The idea for this jacket, both in shape and certain colours, derives from a piece of woven cloth worn by horsemen.*'

All the patterns in this book contain general information (Sizes, Materials, Tension), written and/or charted instructions and details of how to assemble the garment. Everything is presented in a logical order; it is important that you read the pattern through before you start knitting so that you have a general understanding of the work.
The information here relates to reading the patterns section by section and describes the techniques that are used consistently.

SIZES

The patterns are usually written in a range of sizes; instructions for the first size are given outside a set of square brackets, [ ], with the larger sizes following on in order within the brackets.
Look at the *actual* measurement when choosing the size to make. Some garments have a generous amount of 'ease', so you may prefer to knit a smaller size than normal if the finished result is too large for your taste.
Once you have decided on a size, mark the relevant figures throughout the pattern to avoid confusion.

MATERIALS

In this book the designs are all knitted in Rowan yarns – the names and shades of which are quoted with the individual instructions. To avoid the frustration of being unable to obtain specific yarns there is a table of generic equivalents (any standard 4 ply, double knitting, etc) on page 143. Only substitute a different yarn after first making a tension swatch and checking that the number of stitches and rows is the same as the original.
Changing yarns could mean that you will need more or less yarn than stated in the pattern, even though both yarns may be packaged in the same weight balls. Due to the composition of the fibres each type of yarn has a different metreage (yardage) – the actual length of yarn in each ball. Therefore the actual amounts quoted in the pattern can only be used as a guide.
Many of the designs in this book use a number of different colours, some in very small quantities. Yarns are frequently only available in 50g (2oz) balls which means that there is a lot left. Extra yarn may be welcome for future projects, but if you want to be more economical take advantage of the kits being offered for various garments (see page 143). The yarns included in a kit are wound off in more accurate quantities with little wastage.

TENSION

The tension quoted in a pattern has been achieved by the designer of the garment who uses it to make all the stitch and row

calculations. As the tension of your work is personal to you, and to ensure that your sweater finishes up the size that you intended, you *must* make a tension swatch before starting work.
Using the yarn and needles stated and working in the appropriate stitch or pattern, knit a swatch about 15cm (6in) square. Place the finished swatch on a padded surface, gently smooth it into shape, then secure the edges with pins placed at right angles to the fabric.

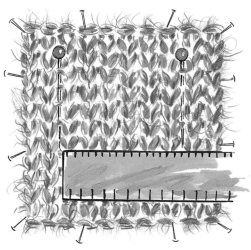

Measuring the stitch tension.

With pins as markers at each end, measure out 10cm (4in) horizontally across the centre of the swatch for the stitch tension; or vertically down the swatch for the row tension. Fewer stitches than stated means that your work is too loose and you need to try again with smaller needles; more stitches than stated indicates that you are knitting too tightly and should try again with larger

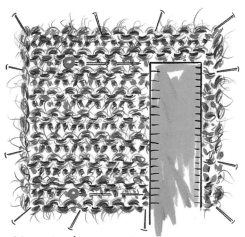

Measuring the row tension.

needles. Changing the needle size is not important as long as you obtain the correct number of stitches and rows to 10cm (4in).

CHARTS

Many designs in this book involve intarsia knitting which is a form of creating colour patterns usually against a background of stocking stitch. To see how the design evolves, sections of a garment are often shown as charts.
The charts are based on a grid of squares; reading horizontally across the grid each square represents a stitch, and vertically up the grid squares indicate the rows of knitting. Symbols represent the various colours: if you find it difficult to 'read' the symbols, photocopy the chart and shade the squares in the appropriate colours. It is also possible to enlarge a chart, if the grid is too small, by using the special facility on a photocopier. Solid lines show the markings for various sizes as well as indicating shaping such as armholes or neck. Only use the lines as a guide for placing the pattern; always follow the written detailed instructions for shaping.

MAKING AN OPEN INCREASE (Yo)

An open increase, known as 'yarn over' and abbreviated as 'yo', is made by putting the yarn over the needle between two stitches; this creates a hole (for buttonholes or decorative, lacy effects) when it is worked on the following row. Exactly how the yarn is placed over the needle depends on the stitches at either side.
Increasing between two knit stitches – at the appropriate position bring the yarn forward to the front of the work between two needles. Knit the next stitch in the usual way.
Increasing between a knit and a purl stitch – work to the position of the increase, then bring the yarn forward to the front between the two needles. Now take the yarn over the top of the right-hand needle point and round to the front again between the two needles. Purl the next stitch in the usual way.
Increasing between a purl and a knit stitch – when you reach the position of the increase, you will see that the yarn is already at the front of the work from purling the previous stitch. Instead of taking the yarn to the back, as you would normally do before knitting, simply proceed to knit the stitch. As you do this, you automatically bring the yarn over the needle so creating an extra loop.
Increasing between two purl stitches – take the yarn completely round the right-hand needle point and to the front again between the two needles. The yarn is now in position to purl the next stitch.

KNITTING WITH COLOUR

There are two main methods of working with colour – Fair Isle knitting and intarsia. Fair Isle work generally involves using two or more colours, with no more than a few stitches between them, repeating across a row of knitting. Intarsia uses small or separate balls of yarn for isolated areas of colour or individual motifs.

Stranding yarns across a purl row.

Fair Isle In Fair Isle knitting, where two colours are used in one row, the yarn not in use is stranded across the back of the work as long as it passes no more than five stitches. On a knit row work the required number of stitches in one colour, then take up the second colour and work with that – and so on – stranding the yarns across the back of the work. Keep the strands fairly loose without them forming a loop; if you pull the yarns across too tightly the work will pucker and the knitting loses its elasticity.

Stranding yarns across a knit row.

On a purl row, work in the same way, allowing the strands to form across the front of the work.
If the yarn must pass over more than five stitches avoid long, loose strands at the back

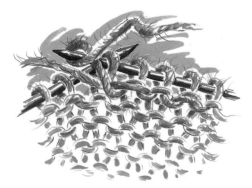

Weaving yarns across the back.

140

of the work by weaving it over and under the working yarn every three or four stitches.
Intarsia When working an isolated area of colour or a motif, use a separate length of yarn or wind off a small ball (depending on the size of the motif) for each area of colour. It is important to link each colour to the next by twisting the yarns together on the wrong side of the work when you change colour – otherwise the different areas of colour separate.

Linking yarns when changing colour.

MAKING UP

After the many hours that it takes to complete a knitted garment, do not spoil the finished effect by rushing the final stages. First make sure that all the loose ends of yarn are secured to prevent them unravelling later on. Always leave a long end of yarn for darning in when you start a new ball of yarn. Thread the end into a blunt-ended wool needle and neatly weave it into the back of the knitting behind the stitches of the same colour. Trim the loose end close the fabric.
For sewing up the garment use matching yarn in the main colour and a blunt-ended wool needle. If the original yarn is unsuitable for sewing up (ie. too thick or textured) choose a similar colour in a finer, smooth quality.

Blocking and Pressing
For a perfect fit the finished pieces of knitting should be blocked (ie. pinned out to the measurements indicated in the diagrams) and pressed according to the specific instructions given on the yarn label. Blocking requires a padded surface. Lay a folded blanket on a table and cover it with a sheet. Place the knitted pieces right side down on the sheet and smooth them out to the correct measurements. Check that the fabric is not distorted and that the lines of stitches and rows are straight, then secure to the pad using pins placed at right angles to the edge of the knitting. For most natural fibres cover the knitting with a damp cloth and, using a warm iron, place it gently on the fabric and lift it up again – without moving the iron in a continuous action. Allow the knitting to dry completely before removing the pins.
Do not press any areas of ribbing or stitch work patterns where the texture of the knitting can easily be damaged.

Backstitch Seam
The most popular seam in common use, the backstitch seam gives a strong firm finish to

most edges, but forms a ridge on the inside of the garment. To work the seam place the pieces to be joined with right sides together and matching any patterns row for row and stitch for stitch. Work in backstitch along the seam, close to the edge, sewing into the centre of each row or stitch to correspond with the row or stitch on the opposite edge.

Invisible Seam
This is a very useful seam when working with thick yarns where a backstitch seam would be too bulky. The seam is virtually undetectable from the right side of the work – the only sign is a slight ridge on the inside of the garment. Place the pieces to be joined edge to edge with the right sides facing upwards. By sewing under the horizontal strands (linking the edge stitch and the following stitch) of alternate edges the two pieces are gradually 'laced' together from the right side.

Overcast Seam
Although the seam is worked through two edges placed together, when it is opened out it lies completely flat. Use an overcast seam for areas of ribbing such as welts and cuffs, or for attaching front bands and collars. With the right sides of the two pieces to be joined together and matching stitches and rows, insert the needle behind the knot of the edge stitch on one side, then through the same part of the corresponding stitch on the second side. Draw the yarn through and repeat these actions to join each pair of row ends.

CARE OF HANDKNITTING

The majority of yarns used in this book are made up of natural fibres; all of them can be hand-washed or dry-cleaned in certain solvents, but only the cotton yarns are suitable for machine-washing. Follow the washing instructions printed on the ball band or label.

Hand-washing
Use hand-warm water in which a mild soap has been dissolved. Never allow the garment to soak, or rub it in the water, as the fabric will become felted. Instead gently squeeze the knitting, supporting it all the time so that the weight of the water does not pull the garment out of shape. Rinse in several changes of water until there is no trace of soap, then spin dry for a short time only.
Never tumble dry a knitted garment or hang it up to dry. Smooth the garment gently into shape and leave it to dry on a flat surface covered with a towel.

Machine-washing
It is possible to machine-wash some cotton yarns on a gentle cycle, but always refer to the instructions with the yarn.
Rowan-Den-m-nit Cotton is indigo dyed and possesses the same unique features as denim jeans. It will shrink with the first wash and continue to fade with subsequent washes. Where this yarn has been used, the making up instructions give details of washing the knitted pieces before they are assembled.

Hints for American Knitters

The patterns in this book should be easy for American knitters to follow. In case of difficulties the following tables and glossaries offer guidance.

TERMINOLOGY

UK	US
cast off	bind off
cont without shaping	work straight
colour	shade
ball band	yarn label
double crochet	single crochet
slip stitch in position	tack down
stocking stitch	stockinette stitch
tension	gauge
treble	double crochet
triple treble	double treble

The following table shows the approximate yarn equivalents in terms of thickness. Always check the tension of substitute yarns before buying sufficient to complete the garment.

UK	US
four-ply	sport
double knitting	knitting worsted
Aran-weight	fisherman
chunky	bulky

METRIC CONVERSION TABLES

Length (to the nearest ¼in)				Weight (rounded up to the nearest ¼oz)	
cm	in	cm	in	g	oz
1	½	55	21¾	25	1
2	¾	60	23½	50	2
3	1¼	65	25½	100	3¾
4	1½	70	27½	150	5½
5	2	75	29½	200	7¼
6	2½	80	31½	250	9
7	2¾	85	33½	300	10¾
8	3	90	35½	350	12½
9	3½	95	37½	400	14¼
10	4	100	39½	450	16
11	4¼	110	43½	500	17¾
12	4¾	120	47	550	19½
13	5	130	51¼	600	21¼
14	5½	140	55	650	23
15	6	150	59	700	24¾
16	6¼	160	63	750	26½
17	6¾	170	67	800	28¼
18	7	180	70¾	850	30
19	7½	190	74¾	900	31¾
20	8	200	78¾	950	33¾
25	9¾	210	82¾	1000	35½
30	11¾	220	86½	1200	42¼
35	13¾	230	90½	1400	49¼
40	15¾	240	94½	1600	56½
45	17¾	250	98½	1800	63½
50	19¾	300	118	2000	70½

NEEDLE SIZE CONVERSION TABLE

Use the needle sizes quoted in the patterns as recommended starting points for making a tension sample. The needle size actually used should be that on which you achieve the stated tension.

Metric	US	Old UK
2mm	0	14
2¼mm	1	13
2½mm		
2¾mm	2	12
3mm		
3¼mm	3	10
3½mm	4	
3¾mm	5	9
4mm	6	8
4½mm	7	7
5mm	8	6
5½mm	9	5
6mm	10	4
6½mm	10½	3
7mm		2
7½mm		1
8mm	11	0
9mm	13	00
10mm	15	000

ABBREVIATIONS

alt – alternate
beg – begin(ning)
ch – chain
cm – centimetres
cont – continue(ing)
dc (sc) – double crochet (single crochet)
dec – decrease(ing)
foll – follow(ing)
g – grams
in – inch(es)
K – knit
K-wise – knitwise

ml – make one stitch by picking up horizontal loop between stitches and knitting into the back of it
mm – millimetres
P – purl
patt – pattern
psso – pass slipped stitch over
rem – remain(ing)
rep – repeat
RS – right side
sl – slip
sp(s) – spaces(s)

ss – slip stitch
st(s) – stitch(es)
st st – stocking (stockinette) stitch
tbl – through back of loop(s)
tog – together
tr (dc) – treble (double crochet)
tr tr (d tr) – triple treble (double treble)
WS – wrong side
yfwd – yarn forward
yo – yarn over (needle)

THE ROWAN STORY

We are proud to announce the publication of *The Original Annabel Fox* and *The Kim Hargreaves Collection*. The first two **Rowan-Anaya Originals**, they combine outstanding knitting design with the range and quality of Rowan Yarns.

Rowan is a Yorkshire-based yarn marketing and design company whose name has become synonymous with the revolution that has swept the needlecraft and handkitting industry and changed its image and practice forever. Gone are the limited colours and synthetics offered by most other spinners; we have created a whole new generation of exciting natural-fibre yarns – from kid silk to chenille – in a myriad colours.

Working with the cream of contemporary designers, including Kaffe Fassett, Edina Ronay and Susan Duckworth, Rowan Yarns commissions special handknitting and needlepoint collections, taking what was once a hobby into the realms of high fashion. Rowan's design collections are now in fashion journals worldwide, while every glossy home supplement bears tasteful evidence of Rowan's artistic craftwork.

Home for Rowan is an old stone mill in a narrow green valley in the shadow of the Pennines overlooking Holmfirth. Rowan Yarns was set up just over thirteen years ago by myself and my colleague Simon Cockin. From the beginning our aims were different from our competitors. We took our palette of yarns to top designers; we worked with them to create yarns in colours to match their specific requirements. Some have proved so popular they have become a permanent part of the Rowan range.

Our yarns are now marketed worldwide and the sheer appeal of the variety and subtlety of colours and textures, combined with our willingness to experiment, ensure our continuing success.

Rowan-Anaya Originals set new standards in quality from the very best contemporary designers. The books are produced with the same care and attention that is given to our yarns and the same eye for form and colour that has been our lifelong hallmark.

We hope that you will enjoy this new range of original designs using Rowan's yarns.

Stephen Sheard.

KITS AND SUPPLIERS

The Rowan yarns used for designs throughout
this book are named in each pattern and can
be obtained from stockists of good quality
knitting yarns.
In case of difficulty, write to the addresses
below for a list of stockists in your area or
consult the yarn list here before substituting a
generic equivalent.

Heavy 4-ply wool	– Rowan Lightweight Double Knitting
Double knitting wool	– Rowan Designer Double Knitting, Rowan Foxtweed Double Knitting, Rowan Lambswool Tweed
Aran-weight	– Rowan Magpie
4-ply yarn	– Rowan Wool and Cotton
4-ply cotton	– Rowan Sea Breeze, Rowan Cabled Mercerised Cotton
Heavy 4-ply cotton	– Rowan Cotton Glacé
Double knitting cotton	– Rowan Handknit Double Knitting Cotton, Rowan Fine Cotton Chenille, Rowan Den-m-nit

United Kingdom
Rowans Yarns, Green Lane Mill, Holmfirth,
West Yorkshire HD7 1RW.
Tel 0484 681881
Fax 0484 687920

USA
Kenneth Bridgewater, Westminster Trading
Corporation, 5 Northern Boulevard, Amherst,
New Hampshire 03031.
Tel 603 886 5041
Fax 603 886 1056

Canada
Christopher Peacock, Estelle Designs and
Sales Ltd, Units 65/67, 2220 Midland
Avenue, Scarborough, Ontario M1P 3ES.
Tel 416 298 9922
Fax 416 298 2429

Australia
Ron Mendelsohn, Sunspun Enterprises PTY
Ltd, 191 Canterbury Road, Canterbury 3126,
Victoria.
Tel 03 830 1609
Fax 03 816 9590

West Germany
Minke Heistra, Textilwerkstatt,
Friedenstrasse 5, 3000 Hanover 1.
Tel 0511 818001
Fax 0511 813108

Germany
Naturwolle Fritzsch, Gewerbepark
Dogelmuhle, 6367 Karben 1.
Tel 060 39 2071
Fax 060 39 2074

Denmark
Sonja Kristensen, Designer Garn, Aagade 3,
Roerbaek, O Hobro.
Tel & Fax 9855 7811

Holland
Henk & Henrietta Beukers, Dorpsstraat 9,
5327 AR Hurwenen.
Tel 04182 1764
Fax 04182 2532

New Zealand
John Q Goldingham Ltd, PO Box 45083,
Epuni Railway, Lower Hutt.
Tel 04 5674 085
Fax 04 5697 444

Norway
Jorun Sandin, Eureka, PO Box 357, 1401 Ski.
Tel 09 871 909

Japan
Mr Iwamoto, Diakeito Co Ltd,
1-5-23 Nakatsu Kita-Ku, Osaka 531.
Tel 06 371 5657

Sweden
Eva Wincent Gelinder, Wincent,
Luntmarkargaten 56, 113 58 Stockholm.
Tel 08 327 060
Fax 08 333 171

Italy
Daniella Basso, La Compagnia Del Cotone,
Via Mazzini 44, 10123 Torino.
Tel 011 878 381
Fax 011 957 4096

Belgium
Studio Hedera, Diestsestraat 172,
B - 3030 Leuven.
Tel 016 232 189

Singapore
Francis Kiew, Classical Hobby House, 1 Jln
Anak Bukit, No B2-15 Bukit Timah Plaza,
Singapore 2158.
Tel 4662179
Fax 7762134

Mexico
Moses Semaria, Estembresy Tejidos Finos
S.A.D. C.V., A.V Michoacan 30 – A, Local 3
Esq Av Mexico, Col Hipodromo Condesa
06170, Mexico 11.
Tel 2 64 84 74

Iceland
Malin Orlyggsdottir, Stockurinn, Orlygsdottir,
Kjorgardi, Laugavegi 159, 101 Reykjavik.
Tel 010 354 1 18258

Finland
Helmi Vuorelma – Oy, Vestjarven Katu 13,
SF – 15141 Lahti.
Tel 010 358 (918) 268 31
Fax 010 358 (918) 517 918

ROWAN KITS

Write to the Rowan distributors above for a
list of stockists of the following designs:
Quizo (page 8)
Alexander Rose (page 33)

The following suppliers have also been used
for yarns and beads. Please contact them
directly for stockist or mail order information.

Texere White Gold (see Gold Dragon, page
21) Texere Yarns, College Mill, Barkerend
Road, Bradford, West Yorkshire, BD3 9AQ.
Tel 0274 722191

Beads
The Bead Shop, 43 Neal Street,
Covent Garden, London WC2H 9PJ.
Tel 071 240 0931

ACKNOWLEDGEMENTS

My special thanks to all the people who have helped me to complete this book. To Ray Moller who, with like-minded vision, produced the beautiful photographs. To Stephen Sheard and Mike Wicks of Rowan Yarns and Carey Smith of Anaya Publishers for their belief in my directing the shoot and their encouragement throughout, my editor Margaret Maino for her patience, Marilyn Wilson for her pattern checking and to David Fordham for his perfectionism.

A big 'thank you' to all my knitters – Sandra Hipperson, Mrs Bradford, Jill Duffy, Pat Rawlinson and her circle, Lynne Wordingham, Mrs North, Mrs Leach, Barbara Wood, Lorna Giles, Mary Oliver, Elaine Clark, Jenny Leigh, Ann Fuller, Ivy Woods, Hilda Clark, Christine Purcell, Miss Wadman, Sue Westgate, Diana Clark, Edna Fox, Patricia Al-Husari and M Burglin – who all knitted the garments for this book.

Finally, thank you to Sarah Heron, my assistant for the last three years, for her enthusiasm and dedication, and to all my family and friends.

A.F.

CREDITS

Clothes and accessories were lent by the following suppliers: *adults' clothes* – Margaret Howell, Neal St East and Paul Smith; *children's clothes* – Nipper; *jewellery* – Neal St East; *horses* – Michel and Pascal Cherfa, Adseem, Abbaye Médiévale, Lagrasse.

Hair and make-up: Jain Berry.
Models: Tijan Winters, Monica Hayes, Mark, Richard, William and Pam Bagguley, Amanda, Annabel, Thomas and Frances Heron, Brigit Marnier, Annabel Fox.

Photograph on page 142 by Andrew Sanderson.